JAMES SWAN, CHĀ-TIC

of the Northwest Coast

DRAWINGS AND WATERCOLORS
FROM THE FRANZ & KATHRYN STENZEL COLLECTION
OF WESTERN AMERICAN ART

By George A. Miles

The Beinecke Rare Book & Manuscript Library

Yale University

Distributed by

University Press of New England

This book accompanies the exhibition
James Swan, Chā-tic of the Northwest Coast
at the Beinecke Rare Book & Manuscript Library
Yale University, New Haven, Connecticut
April 18–July 19, 2003.

JACKET FRONT
"Tomahnawos board at the base of monument
over 'Swell,' a Makah chief buried at Baadah Pt. Neah Bay W.T."
[April 1861?] (page 79)

HALF TITLE
Indian ceremonial dancer (page 95)

TITLE PAGE
"Waadah Island" and "Baadah Point, Neeah Bay." 1859 (pages 68–69)

Library of Congress Cataloging-in-Publication Data

Miles, George A.
   James Swan, Chā-tic of the Northwest Coast : drawings and watercolors
from the Franz & Kathryn Stenzel collection of western American art /
By George A. Miles.
      p. cm.
   ISBN 0-8457-3147-5
   1. Swan, James—Exhibitions. 2. Northwest, Pacific—In art—Exhibitions.
3. Indians in art—Exhibitions. 4. Stenzel, Franz—Art collections—
Exhibitions. 5. Stenzel, Kathryn M. (Kathryn Mathison)—Art collections—Exhibi-
tions. 6. Art—Private collections—Northwest, Pacific—Exhibitions. 7. Art—Con-
necticut—New Haven—Exhibitions. 8. Yale Collection of Western
Americana—Exhibitions. I. Swan, James. II. Stenzel, Franz.
III. Stenzel, Kathryn M. (Kathryn Mathison) IV. Title.

   N6537.S963A4 2003
   759.13—dc21
                     2003004946

ISBN 0-8457-3147-5

PRINTED IN THE UNITED STATES OF AMERICA

Contents

Introduction: The Franz & Kathryn Stenzel Collection of Northwestern Art

The watercolors and drawings reproduced in this exhibition catalog represent a small part of an extraordinary collection given to the Yale Collection of Western Americana in 1997 by Franz and Kathryn Stenzel of Portland, Oregon. Their gift of 1300 oil paintings, watercolors, pastels, pen and ink drawings, pencil sketches, engravings, etchings, lithographs, and photographs depicting the people, places, and history of the Pacific Northwest was the largest donation received by the Western Americana Collection since Frederick W. Beinecke's bequest in 1970. Along with the original art, the Stenzels donated their extensive research collection, which contains files on more than 1,000 artists who worked in the American and Canadian Wests, and their library of more than 1,600 rare and scholarly works concerning Western art.

Private collectors like the Stenzels lie behind many of America's great museum and library collections. Yale librarians are particularly fond of attributing the school's creation in 1701 to the reputed donation of forty folios by ten ministers who gave them "for the founding of a College." George W. Pierson's *The Founding of Yale: The Legend of the Forty Folios* explores the reality behind Yale's creation myth, and while it exposes the flimsy evidence for the specific donation, it reveals that multiple gifts of books over several decades were indeed an essential element in the school's origin. A century later, following the British destruction of the Capitol during the War of 1812, the acquisition of Thomas Jefferson's personal library reinvigorated the Library of Congress and laid the basis for what is now seen, in fact if not in law, as our national library. In 1870, New York City philanthropist James Lenox incorporated his personal library as a free public library. Twenty-five years later the Lenox Library became a cornerstone of the New York Public Library. From Providence, Rhode Island to San Marino, California collectors like John Carter Brown, Edward Ayer, and Henry Huntington supplied the nucleus for new, independent research libraries. The Yale Collection of Western Americana itself arose from the donation to Yale by William Robertson Coe of his rare books, manuscripts, and original art. In each case, collections that reflected the personal passions of individuals inspired the creation of institutions dedicated to preserving the historical record and making it available for a broader audience to study and appreciate.

The dynamic relationship between private collectors and institutions is reflected in this catalog and the exhibition it records. Through it, the Beinecke Library seeks not only to express our respect for the role the Stenzels have played in finding and preserving the visual heritage of the Pacific Northwest but also to inform scholars, teachers, and students about the collection and the opportunities it presents for investigation. Over forty years ago, commenting on the first major exhibition of their then infant collection, the Stenzels observed that few people understood the range or value of the region's pictorial traditions. "Much has been lost or irreparably damaged through fire, dampness, or human carelessness."[1] Through their efforts, much was rediscovered, repaired, and reintroduced to public view. The Yale Collection of Western Americana is honored to record and preserve their accomplishment.

A native of Washington state, Franz Stenzel graduated from Bates College in 1933 and from Harvard Medical School in 1938. He also studied at the Alliance Française in Paris and the University of Berlin. Following World War II he returned to Portland, opened a medical practice, and married Kathryn Marie Mathison. The couple began collecting Western art in 1955 after a patient gave Dr. Stenzel a painting. Over the next forty years, they amassed a collection that eventually included more than 2,500 works. From the beginning, they regarded paintings and drawings as both art and document. Sensitive to aesthetic considerations, they also recognized the broad cultural significance of visual images in nineteenth and early twentieth century America. The Stenzels collected lithographic "birds' eye views" of cities as well as large oil paintings of dramatic natural landscapes. They acquired the work of distinguished Canadian artists alongside the sketchbooks and paintings of American naval officers and government officials. They valued caricatures as well as finished portraits. Unconventional in the breadth of media and range of artists they collected, the Stenzels integrated their diverse collection by focusing on images which depicted the Northwest, its history, and its people.

If the composition of the Stenzels' collection transcended traditional practices, so too did the way they acquired material. Their library demonstrates their familiarity with

auction and gallery sales of the time, but they purchased few pieces through the traditional channels of the art market. They spent more time uncovering material in second-hand stores, antique shops, and private homes. They identified artists who had worked in the Northwest, visited towns where the artists had worked or lived, and wrote to descendants to learn about the artists and find paintings, drawings, and sketches that were often unknown to scholars. Librarians and archivists too often label collectors as competitors rather than collaborators in preserving the past, but no library or museum could have dedicated the time and energy the Stenzels expended finding and acquiring art, books, and manuscripts. "Collecting" is too casual a description for their activity. They hunted, they pursued, they rescued Northwestern images from obscurity.

The watercolors and drawings reproduced in this catalog, made and commissioned by James Gilchrist Swan, comprise the largest group of material by a single artist in the Stenzel collection, but it is a measure of their accomplishment that Swan's art is only one of many important subsets within the collection. There are, for instance, seventy-eight watercolors and drawings by James Madison Alden (1834–1922), a naval officer and artist attached to the Coast Survey of the Pacific shore on board the U. S. S. Steamer *Active* and later a member of the Northwest Boundary Commission. Obtained primarily from Alden family members, all but ten of the pieces date from Alden's service on the Pacific coast between 1854 and 1860. They depict scenes in British Columbia, California, Oregon, and Washington Territory, particularly along the Columbia and Fraser Rivers, and in Yosemite Valley.

Another extensive gathering consists of ninety-one drawings, watercolors, prints, and etching plates by Portland

1 *Early Days in the Northwest* (Portland, 1959), p. 4

artist William Forsyth McIlwraith (1867-1940), who drew many landmarks in and around the city, especially along its waterfront. One of McIlwraith's best known images, "Indians Salmon Fishing at Celilo," is represented by a pencil drawing, a watercolor, three etchings, and three etching plates. Portland was also the principal subject of Herbert Heywood (1893-1969), who is represented by a collection of nineteen prints. Together, the McIlwraith and Heywood images provide a graphic record of the industrial transformation of Portland in the early twentieth century.

The Stenzels' view of the Northwest was not limited to the Willamette and Columbia valleys. They ranged northward to the Alaskan coast and eastward to the continental divide. The collection includes twenty watercolors of Aleuts and Alaskan scenes by Joseph W. Kehoe (1890-1959), a jurist and representative in the Alaskan legislature who was, for a time, acting governor of Alaska. Forty-five pieces by the Wyoming artist Hans Kleiber, who was born in Germany in 1897, depict scenes on the overland trail as well as birds of Wyoming. The Stenzels also recognized that regional commercial networks connected the Pacific Northwest to the southern Pacific. Twenty-four watercolors and drawings by San Francisco painter Daniel Winters (1834-1883) depict scenes in the Sandwich Islands, Society Island, South Island, and Australia that he prepared on assignment for Leslie's *Illustrated London News*.

The Stenzels built significant collections of material by artists who specialized in regional social themes. Cowboy life, a popular topic for western artists since the late nineteenth century, is particularly well represented. Of seventeen works by Gutzon Borglum (1867-1941), best known as the artist who designed and executed Mount Rushmore, ten are drawings of horses or mounted riders. Cowboys also appear in works by Bob Hall, a cowboy and miner born in 1895 whom the Stenzels

came to know personally. The collection includes thirty-four of his drawings and prints as well as thirty-four comic and western postcards. There are thirteen watercolors, drawings, and etchings by Pete Martinez, a cowboy artist who worked on one of Nevada's largest cattle ranches, the Union Land and Cattle Company, in the early twentieth century. Martinez rose from cowhand to foreman, all the while sketching scenes of cowboy life.

Among artists represented by multiple works depicting Native Americans are Irving R. Bacon, E. A. Burbank, A. W. Best, and E. S. Paxson. There is an extensive collection of the editorial cartoons of Pulitzer Prize winner Lute Pease. There are three watercolors of western Canada by Thomas Mower Martin, a watercolor by James Henry Moser, a self-portrait attributed to John Mix Stanley, two paintings by James Everett Stuart, seven watercolors by Peter Peterson Toft, six watercolors and one pen-and-ink drawing by Charles Erskine Scott Wood, as well as a sketchbook made at King Ranch, Texas, in 1938-39 by Alexander Phimister Proctor. The Stenzels once owned thirty pieces by Cleveland Rockwell, but only one Rockwell painting, *In the Rocky Mountains*, remained in the collection when it came to Yale. There are also works by Maynard Dixon, Manning de Villaneuve Lee, N. Plonnin, Frank Earle Schoonover, Olaf Wieghorst, and James Everett Stuart.

The Stenzels' interest in art encompassed book illustration as well as painting and drawing. In addition to prints after John Webber, George Catlin, and Thomas Moran, the collection includes nineteen prints depicting Aleuts and Eskimos from Giulio Ferrario's rare work, *Il Costume Antico e Moderne..: America* (Firenze: V. Batelli, 1826-1828), an extensive collection of prints from the transcontinental railroad surveys, and more than eighty prints from Albert G. Walling's *History of Southern Oregon, comprising Jackson, Josephine, Douglas, Curry and Coos Counties* (Portland, Or., 1884). Additional prints are from *Harper's Weekly, The Illustrated London News, San Francisco Examiner Art Supplement, San Francisco News Letter, Sportsman Review, Truth,* and T*he West Shore*. Finally there are more than four dozen "bird's-eye views" of British Columbia, California, Colorado, Idaho, Minnesota, Montana, Oregon, and Washington cities and towns dating from 1860 to 1959.

At the same time that the Stenzels collected art they assiduously collected information about Western artists. Their research files, maintained as a distinct archive within the Yale Collection of Western Americana, include approximately 6,000 typescript carbons of their outgoing correspondence. Letters to institutions, to scholars, to artists or their descendants and relatives document the Stenzels' pursuit of information about the artists and art they collected. The Stenzels cast a wide net in tracking down information about obscure artists, as can be seen in the many letters written to people who shared an artist's last name and lived in the city of an artist's last known residence.

For the most part, the Stenzels organized their incoming correspondence to facilitate their study of Northwestern artists. Their research files include twenty-three boxes of material for a projected book entitled "Art of the Oregon Country," which was to focus on artists born prior to 1901 working in Oregon, Washington, Idaho, Montana, Wyoming, southern British Columbia, and southern Alberta. The boxes contain files on over 1,000 artists, many of whom are represented by pieces of art in their collection. The files contain notes, printed material, correspondence, and ephemera. Many of them feature letters to the Stenzels from artists or their descendants.

On occasion, the Stenzels acquired original manuscripts of important artists. Although the Stenzel collection includes no paintings by Jervis McEntee (1828-1891), it does contain a group of letters to McEntee from fellow artists George Henry Boughton, Sanford Robinson Gifford, Eastman Johnson, and Worthington Whittredge. In a letter of July 15, 1866, Whittredge describes in detail a trip to the Rocky Mountains. The collection also includes original papers belonging to James Swan, E. S. Paxson, and Lute Pease, as well as extensive correspondence with the descendants of James Madison Alden.

Throughout the time they were active collectors, the Stenzels shared their art, their research, and their insights concerning the early pictorial art of the Northwest with scholars, libraries, museums, and other collectors. Individual pieces from the Stenzels' collection were exhibited broadly, including major shows at the Amon Carter Museum, the Cheney Cowles Memorial Museum in Spokane, the Montana Historical Society, the Oregon Historical Society, the Museum of Art at the University of Oregon, and the Portland Art Museum. In 1973, four Stenzel pieces were the only privately owned art included in the first art exhibit organized by the United States Information Agency to be shown behind the Iron curtain.

Although the Stenzels never published their general study of early Northwestern artists, research for the larger project contributed to in-depth studies of two prominent Northwest artists. *Cleveland Rockwell, Scientist and Artist, 1837-1907* accompanied a major exhibit of the same title at the Oregon Historical Society in 1972. Three years later the Amon Carter Museum in Fort Worth published *James Madison Alden, Yankee Artist of the Pacific Coast, 1854-1860* to accompany an exhibition drawn primarily from the Stenzels' collection. The Alden exhibition traveled to museums in Oklahoma, Oregon, Washington, and Canada before it closed in 1976. The Stenzels also wrote several brief exhibition catalogs including *Early Days in the Northwest* (1959) for the Portland Art Museum, *Art of the Oregon Territory* (1959) for the Museum of Art at the University of Oregon, *An Art Perspective of the Historic Pacific Northwest* (1963) for the Montana Historical Society and the Eastern Washington State Historical Society, *E. S. Paxson, Montana Artist* (1963) for the Montana Historical Society, and *Anton Schonborn: Western Forts* for the Amon Carter Museum (1972).

During more than a quarter century of active collecting, the Stenzels donated many items from their collection to support institutional collections. The C.M. Russell Gallery, the Montana Historical Society, the Oregon Historical Society, and the Alaska State University were all recipients of significant gifts from the Stenzels. In addition, the Stenzels offered 206 works of art for sale at Sotheby's in Los Angeles on June 24, 1980. Detailed descriptions of the Stenzels' art and research collections at Yale, prepared by Diana Smith of the Beinecke Rare Book and Manuscript Library, can be consulted at the Library's web site: http://www.library.yale.edu/beinecke

In their passionate pursuit of Northwestern art, the Stenzels crafted a legacy that will enable generations of students and scholars to investigate the history of the Pacific Northwest and consider the role of the visual arts in American culture. This catalog and the exhibit it accompanies represent the Beinecke Library's commitment to encourage and support the studies that Franz and Kathryn Stenzel have made possible.

James G Swan June 1883

James Swan:
Chā-tic
of the Northwest Coast

In January, 1850 James Gilchrist Swan, a thirty-one-year-old ship chandler and admiralty lawyer, sailed from Boston for San Francisco aboard the *Rob Roy*. Swan's departure transformed his life. He left an estranged wife, two children, and what appears to have been a successful if modest business to pursue uncertain adventure at the western edge of America. Except for occasional, brief visits to Washington, D. C., or to his family in Boston or in his home town of Medford, Massachusetts, Swan spent most of his remaining life on the Olympic Peninsula, the northwestern extreme of Washington Territory. Away from the mercantile routines of the New England waterfront, he pursued a dizzying array of careers. Before he died in 1900, he worked as a steamship purser between San Francisco and Marysville, as an oysterman and customs agent at Shoalwater Bay (a role he played again, a decade later, at Neah Bay), as a botanist, an author, and personal secretary for Territorial Delegate Isaac I. Stevens. Later he wrote columns for San Francisco and Olympia newspapers describing life on Puget Sound, helped run the Makah Indian agency, where he taught school, and served Port Townsend as notary public, pilot commissioner, and federal commissioner for the third judicial district. He became a probate judge, served as justice of the peace, worked undercover to gather economic information for the Northern Pacific Rail Road, collected artifacts for the Smithsonian Institution, and served as consul for the Kingdom of Hawaii at Puget Sound.

Swan's books and articles, including *The Northwest Coast; or Three Years' Residence in Washington Territory* (1857), *The Indians of Cape Flattery* (1869), and *The Haida Indians of the Queen Charlotte Islands, British Columbia* (1874) established his reputation as one of the country's foremost experts on the history and culture of Northwestern Indian communities. He collaborated with Spencer Baird of the Smithsonian Institution and contributed to the works of Henry Schoolcraft, Hubert Howe Bancroft, Garrick Mallory, and Franz Boas. Government officials like William Gouverneur Morris solicited his opinions concerning Indian affairs in Alaska, while Thomas Canfield, director and general agent of the Northern Pacific Railroad, hired him to canvas the Northwest to identify the best terminus for a transcontinental railroad.

Amidst his many "careers," Swan's most remarkable achievement may have been the personal log he maintained daily for the last 41 years of his life, beginning in 1859. These journals, most of which are now at the University of Washington Library, have long marked Swan as one of America's foremost diarists. He was also an avid correspondent, attested to by extensive files at the Smithsonian Institution and at the University of British Columbia.[1] Swan may have shed gladly many Boston customs, but no matter how remote his travels, he always bore with him the literary imprint of a New England education. Contemplating Swan's life, Ivan Doig observed

all the regularity in him is channeled down his right arm into his pen. He may pass from job to job to job with the liquid hops of a squirrel, but his diary account of his days and his record of effort to learn from the Indians are the steadiest kind of achievement.... A scrupulous correspondent, Swan is perpetually eager for mail and often answers instantly, putting the reply on the same mailboat. No question: the stickum that holds his life together is in his inkwell.[2]

Swan's pen and inkwell produced not only words but hundreds of pictures: watercolors of the plants he found along Shoalwater Bay, sketches of Indian villages and the homes of white settlers, copies of Indian designs, paintings of their dances and material culture, as well as sketches of natural wonders he encountered in his travels. In recognition of

Swan's avocation, the Makah Indians of Cape Flattery, among whom he spent many years, bestowed upon him the name *Chā-tic*, meaning the painter.[3]

Although there is no evidence that Swan received formal training as an artist, he clearly carried west the ante-bellum American compulsion to make pictures. He grew up as lithography and power presses revolutionized the role of illustration in popular culture. During the 1830s pictures of all sorts flourished in books and became a staple of American periodicals. Drawing manuals, a century earlier the reading matter of English gentleman, were widely available. Galleries and museums attracted urban audiences throughout the Northeast. Naturalists, ethnographers, engineers, journalists, and civic boosters joined professional artists to swell the ranks of picture makers, and the ability to sketch accurately a person, place, or event became as much a mark of the "educated man" as the ability to write an eloquent letter or persuasive essay. Whether Swan studied with an unknown teacher or trained himself, his penchant for illustrating his diaries, for making complementary visual journals in commercial sketchbooks, and for supplying the illustrations that appeared in his books and essays reflects the enduring impact of a New England upbringing that Swan brought to his engagement with the American frontier.

Ivan Doig contemplated Swan's literary legacy in *Winter Brothers: A Season at the Edge of America*. Lucile McDonald used his diaries to fashion a basic biography in *Swan among the Indians*, and Douglas Cole's *Captured Heritage: The Scramble for Northwest Coast Artifacts* exploited his extensive correspondence with Spencer Baird to explore Swan's major contribu-

---

1 At the Manuscripts, Special Collections, University Archives department of the University of Washington Library the *James G. Swan Papers, 1850-1909*, contains correspondence, diaries, business records, reports, family genealogical material, financial records, and historical writings. At the Rare Books and Special Collections department at the University of British Columbia Library the *James G. Swan Papers, 1852-1900*, contains extensive correspondence that reflects Swan's personal life and professional work as collector of Indian artifacts, as well as cash books and estate records. It also holds the official records of Swan's work as Notary Public, U.S. Commissioner, Pilot Commissioner, Hawaiian Consul, and Commissioner of Oregon. At the Smithsonian Institution, The National Anthropological Archives holds four collections with Swan correspondence: *Records of the Bureau of American Ethnology, letters received, 1879-1888*; *Records of the Bureau of American Ethnology, letters received 1888-1906*; *Letters received from James G. Swan 1878* (Manuscript 1215); and *Papers of John Constantine Pilling 1879-1897*.

2 Ivan Doig, *Winter Brothers: A Season at the Edge of America* (New York, 1980), 162-163.

3 James G. Swan, *The Indians of Cape Flattery, at the Entrance to the Strait of Fuca, Washington Territory* (Washington, 1869), 9.

tions to the Smithsonian Institution's collections.[4] But little has been written about Swan's drawings and watercolors. Although his published works included reproductions of his sketches and paintings and often alluded to the existence of other images in his possession, Swan's pictorial accomplishments have drawn scant attention. A partial answer for this neglect lies in the condition of Swan's finances at his death and the consequent handling of his estate.

The Panic of 1893 shattered the economy of Swan's home, Port Townsend, crushing its commercial and political aspirations. Within a few years the town's population plummeted from 7,000 to 2,000. In his eighties, with his health deteriorating and subject to bouts of heavy drinking, Swan's own fortunes foundered. When he died on May 19, 1900, his debts exceeded his assets. It took his executor, James Seavey, nearly eight years to close the estate as he struggled to meet the claims of as many creditors as possible. Swan's books were sold to Shorey Books of Seattle. A grand-nephew suggested that his diaries, deemed to have no commercial value, be donated to a local library (from which they were transferred to the library at the University of Washington's Seattle campus in 1927). Swan's drawings and a small collection of personal manuscripts were the final assets to be sold. On February 17, 1908, Port Townsend attorney J. A. Kuhn purchased the "Mythological drawings" for $250 and the manuscripts, which included Swan's final diary, for $2. Swan had sent at least eighteen watercolors and drawings to the Smithsonian in the 1880s, but it appears that Kuhn purchased the bulk of Swan's

artistic corpus, at which point the drawings and papers disappeared from the public record for a half century.[5]

Sometime after 1955, Franz and Kathryn Stenzel identified a significant remnant of the Kuhn collection containing over 115 drawings and a small but interesting group of manuscripts that included vocabularies of the Chinook jargon and Makah languages, four censuses of the Makah in the 1860s, a detailed letter from 1879 describing a visit to the Makah at Neah Bay, a synopsis of his trip to the Queen Charlotte Islands in 1883, and Swan's final diary. When they purchased the collection the Stenzels promised not to identify the seller, a promise they have kept ever since. In 1959 they exhibited forty-four of the drawings in *Early Days in the Northwest* at the Portland Art Museum, marking the first and, until now, only major exhibition of Swan's work.[6] The catalog which accompanied the exhibit reproduced nine of the pieces. In 1997 the Stenzels donated their Swan material to the Yale Collection of Western Americana as part of their larger collection of Northwestern art. This catalog reproduces 115 pieces from their Swan collection and attempts to place the works in the context of Swan's life. Far from a final statement on his life or artistic output, it strives to make Swan's work more familiar and to encourage further examination of his career.

It is ironic that a man who spent the last four decades of his life recording his daily, even hourly, experiences seems not

4 Doig, *Winter Brothers*; Lucile McDonald, *Swan Among the Indians: Life of James G. Swan, 1818-1900* (Portland, 1972); Douglas Cole, *Captured Heritage: The Scramble for Northwest Coast Artifacts* (Seattle, 1985).

5 "Documents relating to Swan's estate, 1900-1911," box 11, folder 222, *Franz R. and Kathryn M. Stenzel Collection of Western Art*, Yale Collection of Western Americana, Beinecke Rare Book & Manuscript Library. Franz Stenzel, *Early Days in the Northwest* (Portland, Oregon, 1959), 31 reports that the sale included 250 paintings, but the documents relating to Swan's estate do not enumerate the number of drawings or a unit price; they record only the price for the lot.

6 *Ibid.*, and personal conversations with Kathryn Stenzel.

to have kept an account of his trip to Gold Rush California nor to have made any drawings of his first years on the Pacific Coast. Many of his contemporary argonauts, whether they sailed to San Francisco or trekked overland across the plains and mountains, did keep journals, some of which are heavily illustrated. Perhaps Swan lost his journals and drawings from this period. Perhaps he was too busy to write and draw. Or perhaps his independent, often contrary spirit led him to resist activities that he saw so many around him pursuing. Whatever the case, the record of Swan's pictorial legacy begins only after his departure from San Francisco and arrival at Shoalwater Bay, Oregon Territory, on November 28, 1852. The earliest dated work in the Stenzel collection, a modest watercolor captioned "Species of fungus found at Shoalwater Bay, Oregon," is from December, 1852, no more than a few weeks after Swan's arrival. The latest dated work is a colored-pencil drawing captioned "Black Cod," made July 3, 1884. Many of the originals are undated, and some manuscript captions appear to misdate other pictures, but it is frequently possible to correlate the works with Swan's travels and with specific events he discusses in his journals and letters. The catalog arranges the plates in rough chronological order.

The botany of the Northwest Coast captivated Swan and dominates his earliest surviving work. An avid naturalist who loved to fashion culinary experiments from local foods wherever he traveled, Swan also investigated the medicinal qualities of indigenous plants and the ways Indians used them. The first eleven plates in the catalog (pages 39–46) are botanical watercolors from his days at Shoalwater Bay, where he filed a preemption claim for 315 acres on May 1, 1853, one day before the area became part of the newly created Washington Territory. Botany remained an interest throughout his life. Pages 47

through 53 are watercolors he made while living in Port Townsend or at Neah Bay near Cape Flattery.

Swan dabbled in the oyster business while he lived at Shoalwater Bay, but applied his greatest industry to satisfying his curiosity about the Indians who lived around his new home. Swan attributed his fascination with the Indians of the Northwest Coast to the stories he heard from an uncle who had sailed to Oregon to trade with them decades earlier. His interests were rekindled in 1852 when Chetzamoka, a leader of the Chemakum Indian community at Port Townsend, visited San Francisco. Swan met Chetzamoka, who encouraged Swan to visit his home along the Strait of Juan de Fuca. Swan did not do so until 1859, but from the time he arrived in the Northwest he sought to meet Native Americans, to learn their languages, and to speak with them about their lives, their traditions, and their religious beliefs.[7]

For a middle-class easterner of the mid-nineteenth century, Swan appears unusually sensitive to the variety and particularity of Indian communities. In *The Northwest Coast; or Three Years' Residence in Washington Territory*, he refused to generalize about "Indians" and asserted, "In all matters relating to Indians, I only give an account of those *I have lived with* [original emphasis], the Chenooks, Chehalis, and one or two tribes north of Gray's Harbor."[8] He also criticized literary stereotypes of Indians as distant, stoic, and inhospitable.

Let the Indian once get acquainted, and feel that he is in the presence of a friend and one who feels an interest in his welfare, and he then throws off this reserve, and then it is seen that he can talk and laugh

7 James G. Swan, *The Northwest Coast; or, Three Years Residence in Washington Territory* (New York, 1857), 17.
8 *Ibid.*, vi.

like the rest of the human family. His reserve is most completely thrown off when at home in the midst of his lodge circle, or in seasons of leisure and retirement in the depths of the forest. Then the stranger who may have gained his confidence not only has the opportunity to learn his method of domestic economy, but can hear the relation of those tales and legends which have been handed down from generation to generation, and which the casual visitor or stranger is never permitted to listen to.[9]

Swan demonstrated considerable empathy for Northwestern Indian communities that confronted intruding white frontiersmen and the expansion of American settlements into their homelands. He recognized that the Indians' interest in trading with whites did not mean they wanted to adopt white customs.

They feel as we would if a foreign people came among us, and attempted to force their customs on us whether we liked them or not. We are willing the foreigners should come, and settle, and live with us; but if they attempted to force upon us their language and religion, and make us leave our old homes and take up new ones, we would certainly rebel; and it would only be by a long intercourse of years that our manners could be made to approximate.[10]

Throughout his life, Swan made friends with individual Native Americans and moved easily within their communities. Writing for the *Washington Standard* in November 1861, he attributed his "success" to a rule he always followed, "I never tell an Indian a lie, even in a joke, and I have never since I have been in this Territory, which is since 1852, carried a weapon of defence with me whenever I went among them. I have always found that a civil tongue is the best weapon I can use." Swan acknowledged that he enjoyed a certain freedom in approaching Indians, for his work among them had "always been of a peaceful nature, hence I have no use for pistols, dirks, or knives. I know there are times when such things are not only necessary, but indispensable, but the promiscuous wearing of firearms among Indians during times of peace is more likely to provoke hostility than any thing I know."[11]

The relatively easy access Swan enjoyed among the Indian communities of the Northwest Coast reflects in part the generally peaceful history of Indian-white relations in the region. From the late eighteenth century until the arrival of American settlers in the 1840s, the mutual benefits of commercial exchange led both sides to overlook, if not forget, occasional abuses by the other. American popular culture memorialized Indian destruction of New England vessels and seizure of their crews, but such incidents were clearly exceptional. Similarly, most whites preferred quiet, uneventful trade to warfare with Indians. Hostilities before 1850 were short lived, if intense.[12]

By the 1840s, as American settlers began to arrive in large numbers, epidemic disease had so reduced Indian populations that conflicts over possession of the land were muted. The Rogue River War of 1854–1855 and brief battles along Puget Sound in early 1856 established American control of Oregon's gold fields and commercial harbors along the sound. Elsewhere, Indian and white communities established peaceful

---

9 *Ibid.,* 152–53.
10 *Ibid.,* 368.

11 James G. Swan, *Almost Out of the World; Scenes from Washington Territory: the Strait of Juan de Fuca,* ed. William A. Katz (Tacoma, 1971), 108.
12 Douglas Cole and David Darling, "History of the Early Period," *Handbook of North American Indians; Volume 7: Northwest Coast,* ed. Wayne Suttles (Washington, D. C., 1990), 119–134 and Cesare Marino, "History of Western Washington since 1846," *Ibid.,* 169–179.

if not always amicable understandings of where each would live and how they would share the marine resources of the region. Trade, which once depended upon the annual arrival of sailing vessels off the coast, became an intrinsic part of daily life in the Northwest as each community found it convenient to rely upon the other to provide goods they could not easily produce themselves.

Given Swan's personal diplomatic skills and his intense interest in understanding Indian communities, his appointment as a customs agent on June 9, 1854, seems natural. On the coast of Washington, the principal responsibility of the customs office was to regulate the Indian trade. The seriousness with which Swan took his duties is revealed in the story behind the earliest sketch of an Indian subject in the Stenzel collection (page 55). Swan had resisted for some time invitations by the Quinault Indians to visit their coastal village sixty miles north of his home, but when a Quinault delegation reported that a strange steamer was trading with Indians at Point Grenville, five miles south of their village, Swan made his way overland by foot to investigate whether the Russian American Company or Hudson's Bay Company might be smuggling. When he discovered that the vessel was the *U. S. S. Active*, part of the Coast Survey, Swan concluded the Indians had outfoxed him. Nonetheless, he walked the additional few miles to the Quinault village where he made a sketch that he later reproduced on page 262 of *The Northwest Coast*.[13]

The next winter, Washington governor Isaac Ingalls Stevens asked Swan to join the territorial party that hoped to negotiate a treaty with the Chinook, Quinault, Chehalis, Cowlitz, and Satsop communities of the central Olympic peninsula. In February 1855, the treaty commissioners gath-

ered at the home of Judge Sidney Ford along the Chehalis River (Swan's 1859 sketch of Ford's house is reproduced on page 67). From Ford's home, the party traveled up river to James Pilkington's preemption claim where the council convened on February 25. Swan described the site as a bluff above the south bank of the river, about ten miles from its mouth. His sketch of the treaty grounds, page 57, later appeared on page 336 of *The Northwest Coast*. The parties met for a week but failed to reach an agreement. Swan, who admired Governor Stevens and would soon become his personal secretary, ascribed the failure to Indian frustration with having to wait for Congressional approval before receiving payment for lands they might cede. Historians have been less kind to Stevens, citing his insensitivity to tensions among the Indian communities and his misunderstanding of the importance of particular sites to them as reasons the council failed.[14]

The list of illustrations for *The Northwest Coast* includes at least sixteen plates based on sketches by Swan, but the Stenzel collection contains only three more rough, undated, preliminary sketches that appear to date from Swan's time at Shoalwater Bay. Pages 56, 58, and 153 may be early drafts of sketches that appear on pages 338, 330, and 104 respectively of *The Northwest Coast*. The original art may have been retained by the book's publisher, Harper Brothers, discarded by Swan himself, or lost after his death. As Swan did not always sign his sketches, perhaps they lie unattributed in a private or institutional collection.

After six years on the Pacific coast, Swan returned east in late 1856. Harper Brothers released *The Northwest Coast* the

14 *Ibid.*, 338-351. The standard biography of Stevens is Kent D. Richards, *Isaac I. Stevens: Young Man in a Hurry* (Provo, 1979). Also see Clifford E. Trafzer, ed., *Indians, Superintendents, and Councils: Northwestern Indian Policy, 1850-1855* (Lanham, Md., 1986).

13 Swan, *Northwest Coast*, 250-64.

next year, at the same time that Henry Rowe Schoolcraft published a report from Swan regarding Northwestern Indian religious customs in the sixth and final volume of his encyclopedic *Historical and Statistical Information Respecting the History, Condition, and Prospects of the Indian Tribes of the United States.* Swan was already in Washington, D. C., when Isaac Stevens was elected Congressional delegate from Washington Territory. Swan, who found government service interesting, accepted an offer to become Stevens's personal secretary, but he soon found that Stevens's patronage carried far less weight in Washington, D. C., than it had in Washington Territory.[15]

By the fall of 1858 Swan decided to return west and make his home in Port Townsend at the head of Puget Sound, where he planned to establish a mercantile trade outfitting whalers for work in the north Pacific. Never a man to limit his interests or options, Swan also arranged to serve as columnist and reporter for a San Francisco newspaper, the *Daily Evening Bulletin.* He wrote fourteen columns for the *Bulletin* between May 9, 1859, and October 22, 1860. From 1861 through 1867 he wrote irregularly for the Olympia *Washington Standard* as well as the Olympia *Pioneer and Democrat.* A collection of his newspaper essays, compiled and edited by William A. Katz, was published in 1971 under the title *Almost Out of the World.*[16]

Shortly after arriving in Port Townsend in February 1859, Swan visited Chetzamoka, the Chemakum Indian leader he had met in San Francisco nearly a decade earlier. Chetzamoka, by all accounts, matched Swan's strong, self-confident personality. The Chemakum, like most Northwestern Coast Indian communities, recognized strong social distinctions based on heredity and wealth, and Chetzamoka never hesitated to assert his status. The local white community sarcastically referred to him as the "Duke of York," calling his first, eldest wife "Queen Victoria," and his youngest wife "Jenny Lind." Swan seems to have enjoyed both the man and the fuss. In March he accompanied the Duke and his family on a fishing expedition up Chemakum Creek, five miles from its mouth on Hadlock Bay. The trip exemplified one of the important economic compromises that most regional treaties ratified. When Northwest Coast Indians ceded land, they retained the right to fish and hunt at their accustomed locations. Chetzamoka's favorite spot had become the site of "Hoff's Mill," Swan's sketch of which is reproduced here on page 59.[17]

A few weeks later, Swan's patience and friendship with Chetzamoka provided a special opportunity; he was invited to observe for the first time a Chemakum *tomanawos* ceremony. A Chinook jargon term for a guardian or familiar spirit, *tomanawos* also applied to ceremonies and objects that could harness or direct supernatural power. Swan translated the term as medicine or magic but preferred to use the Chinook jargon term that he heard the Indians speak rather than an English approximation.[18]

---

15 Henry Rowe Schoolcraft, *Historical and Statistical Information Respecting the History, Condition, and Prospects of the Indian Tribes of the United States* (Philadelphia, 1851-1857), volume 6, 632-635. Volume 6 is also entitled *History of the Indian Tribes of the United States: Their Present Condition and Prospects, and a Sketch of Their Ancient Status.* MacDonald, *Swan Among the Indians,* 29-33.

16 *Almost Out of the World,* xxi-xxii.

17 *Ibid.,* 15-17.

18 Swan, who employed a variety of spellings of the word over the years, discussed the concept of *tomanawos* in *The Northwest Coast,* 173 & 420. Swan's manuscript vocabulary in his autograph journal, box 10, folder 191, *Franz R. and Kathryn M. Stenzel Collection of Western Art,* 129, equates *tomanawos* with the Makah term *duqually* and the English words medicine or magic. For further discussion of the term as well as alternate spellings, consult George Gibbs, *A Dictionary of the Chinook Jargon or Trade Language of Oregon* (Washington, 1863), 25 and W. S. Phillips, *The Chinook Book* (Seattle, 1913), 92-94. For a brief overview of the Chinook Jargon, see *The Handbook of North American Indians; Volume 17: Languages,* ed. Ives Goddard (Washington, 1996), 127-130.

Swan described his experience at the ceremony in a long article that appeared in the *Bulletin*. The ceremonies began on Tuesday evening April 26 and continued through Sunday, May 1. On the first night Swan was permitted to enter the lodge to hear the opening chants, but the next morning he learned that despite his friendship with Chetzamoka, parts of the ceremonies remained closed to all non-Indians. Over the next several days, Swan observed the waterfront portion of the ceremonies as well as certain evening dances, but stood outside the lodge during private rites. On Sunday morning, after closing ceremonies were held at water's edge, Chetzamoka and his family began a day long *potlatch*, or distribution of presents to all the Indian participants. Swan used colored pencils to sketch Sunday morning's ceremonies (pages 60 & 61) and added watercolor over pencil to depict "Jenny Lind" distributing presents in her husband's lodge later that day (page 62). The images appear to be the earliest representations of the Chemakum ceremonies.[19]

Unwilling or unable to settle into a merchant's life, Swan spent the spring and early summer of 1859 traveling throughout the Olympic Peninsula. At the end of May he joined Colonel Mike Simmons, the chief agent for Puget Sound, as Simmons visited Indian communities to inform them that Congress had finally approved the treaties they had signed with Governor Stevens in 1855. Swan, who met Simmons years before, referred to him as the Daniel Boone of Washington Territory. First they traveled northwest to the three thousand acre Lummi reservation at Bellingham Bay. On June 1, Swan used colored pencil to sketch the view looking north from the Lummi's principal town (page 63). Leaving Bellingham Bay, the party traveled west to Neah Bay to meet with the Makah,

after which they turned east along the northern coast of the Olympic Peninsula to visit the Clallam. At Clallam Bay they anchored opposite the lodge of Capt. Jack, a prominent leader, whose home became the subject of a Swan pencil sketch (page 64). Shortly after returning to Port Townsend (page 65), Swan left to visit Simmon's home at Skookum Bay (page 66) and Judge Ford on the Chehalis River (page 67).[20]

Of all Swan's trips during the spring and summer of 1859, the most significant were to the Makah reservation at Neah Bay, a few miles east of Cape Flattery at the entrance to the Strait of Juan de Fuca. Swan first visited the Makah in March, shortly after arriving in Port Townsend. Following his brief sojourn there with Simmons in June, he arranged a third visit before the end of summer. On September 14, Swan and Henry Webster, the agent at Neah Bay, left Port Townsend aboard a canoe commanded by a prominent young Makah named Swell. The crew of nine paddled north to Victoria, British Columbia, where the Makah traditionally traded with Indians from the northern coast. The next night, under a full moon with a favorable tide propelling them westward from Victoria to Neah Bay, Swell regaled Swan with Makah stories about the aurora borealis they were enjoying in the northern sky. The next month, in an article published in the Olympia *Pioneer and Democrat*, Swan described Swell as "one of the most intelligent Indians I have ever seen....He is still quite a young man, but if he lives, he is destined to be a man of importance among his own and neighboring tribes."[21]

Whatever thoughts of commerce Swan had brought to Port Townsend probably fell away during his trip with Swell. As it did throughout his life, satisfying his intellectual curios-

19 *Almost Out of the World*, 47-57.

20 *Ibid.*, 60-67.
21 *Ibid.*, 67-73. The description of Swell appears on page 70.

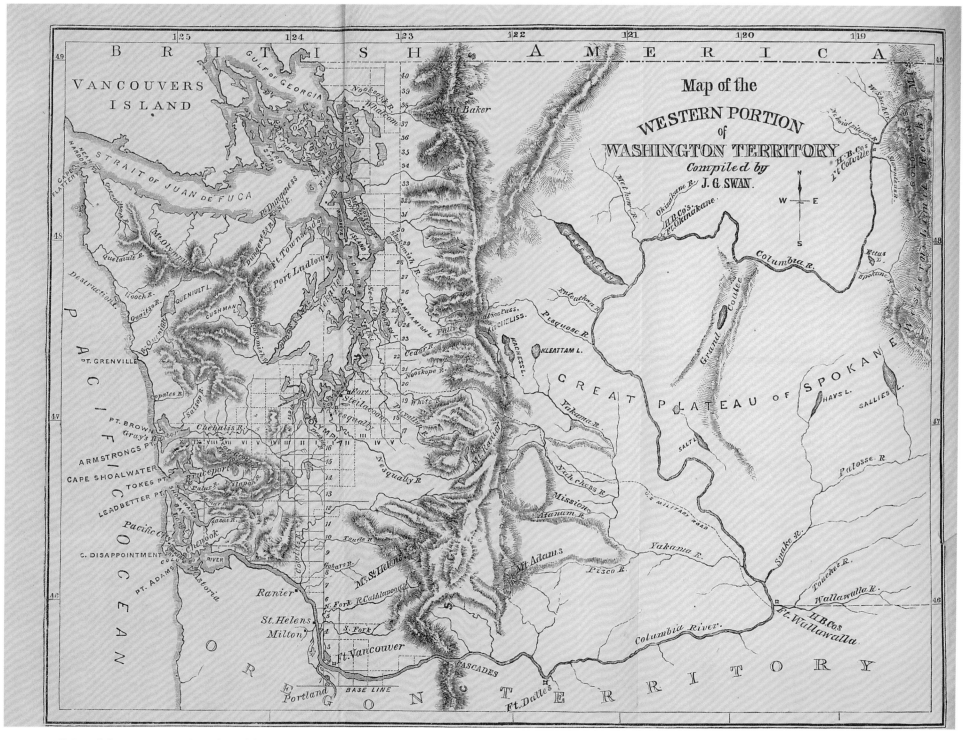

"Map of the western portion of Washington Territory. Compiled by J. G. Swan." From his *The Northwest Coast; or, Three Years Residence in Washington Territory* (1857).

ity triumphed over the practical concern of making a living. He stayed with the Makah for ten days in September and decided to arrange an extended visit. A brief trip to Port Townsend allowed him to settle his affairs, and he returned to Neah Bay in early October, planning to spend two months "seeing something of the habits and customs of the Mackah." At some point among his many visits to Neah Bay, he took the time to create a two-sheet panoramic watercolor of "Waaddah Island" and "Baadah Point, Neah Bay" (pages 68 & 69). He also applied himself enthusiastically to the task of learning the Makah language as well as their material culture, myths, ceremonies, legends, and arts.[22]

Swan recorded his initial impressions of the Makah in a lengthy essay that appeared in the San Francisco *Evening Bulletin* a year later. It is tempting to imagine him writing the article while reviewing the sketches he made during those last months of 1859.

The houses of the Mackahs are built of cedar boards and planks, and are usually of large size, 18 to 20 feet high and from 40 to 60 feet square, with slightly elevated shed-like roofs. They are very comfortable dwellings, and contain several families each. Every family has its separate fire, the smoke of which serves not only to dry the fish and blubber suspended over it, but causes an intense smarting to the eyes of the visitors who are unaccustomed to its acrid fumes. [page 70]

....Around the sides are the sleeping places, and over these, on beams, are the hunting and fishing implements [pages 71, 72, 73]

....In almost every lodge may be seen one or two of the largest-sized boards, carefully smoothed with little chisels, used like a cooper's

adze, called Tomanawos boards. Some that I measured were 25 feet long and 6 feet wide.

The chief or head of each family has painted on his Tomanawos board his particular Hieroglyphics, which are at once the rubrico, or coat-of-arms, or private mark, by which property is designated. These paintings represent the various objects of their mythology [pages 75–79].[23]

The *tomanawos* boards particularly fascinated Swan. Intrigued by their intricate design as well as the graphic identity they represented, Swan began a quarter-century exploration of Northwest Indian crests, totems, and artistic expression. From the home of Yellicom, also known as Flattery Jack, he copied a board depicting the Makah "Thunderbird," reproduced here on page 76. Swan made certain to obtain an explanation of the drawing from his hosts. "The Thunder Bird is an Indian of gigantic proportions, who lives on top of the mountains. His food is whales, and when hungry he puts on his wings and feathers as an Indian wraps himself in a blanket, and sails out in search of his prey." The Thunderbird carries with him a special fish, the Ha-hake-to-ak, which resembles a sea horse. The fish's head is "as sharp as a knife" and its tongue produces lightning. "When a whale is discovered, the Hah-hake-to-ak darts out its fiery tongue, which kills the fish; and as the mighty bird settles down to seize it in its talons, the rustling of its great wings produces the thunder." The bird carried the whale to its mountain home to devour it.[24]

Swan's artistry drew the attention of the Makah, who began to trade artifacts with him in exchange for his drawings. One day a village leader asked Swan to paint a design on his

22 *Ibid.*, 73-86.

23 *Ibid.*, 78.
24 *Ibid.*, 85; *Indians of Cape Flattery*, 8-9.

canoe sail. "He said he wanted a 'Boston' picture, and as he always went faster than any of the other Indians when traveling up and down the Sound in his canoe, he wished me to paint a horse."[25] Later, in his major work on the Makah, *The Indians of Cape Flattery*, Swan reported that he had "painted various devices for these Indians, and have decorated their ta-ma-na-was masks; and in every instance I was simply required to paint something the Indians had never seen before." Swan's nickname among the Makah became *Chā-tic*, the painter.[26]

Swan reciprocated the Makah's interest in his art, asking them to make paintings and drawings for him. Page 77 reproduces a drawing made for Swan by Kitchen-sum on November 10, 1859. Swan's manuscript annotations describe how the Makah made red paint by spitting chewed salmon eggs into vermilion and used ground bituminous coal for black. The drawing itself reproduced the sign with which Kitchen-sum marked his property.

Swan returned to Port Townsend by canoe in late November, carrying with him notes, drawings, and Makah artifacts. On December 28 he met George Suckley, a physician who had served as a naturalist on the Pacific Railway survey under Isaac Stevens. Suckley, who had just published *The Natural History of Washington Territory*, was preparing to send his natural history collection to the Smithsonian Institution, and he encouraged Swan to contribute his Makah artifacts to the national museum. Suckley's recommendation was well timed, for under the leadership of Joseph Henry and Spencer Baird,

the Smithsonian was about to begin an extensive program of collecting ethnographic material related to Native Americans. In 1861 and again in 1863 the museum distributed a circular encouraging government employees and private citizens alike to donate material. Swan soon became its most important contributor from the Northwest Coast.[27]

Swan shuttled up and down the Strait of Juan de Fuca throughout 1860 and 1861. Writing for various newspapers, he found time to collect material for the Smithsonian and to help local Indian agents manage their affairs. On March 1, 1861, his friend Swell was killed by a group of Elwha Indians with whom the Makah had been feuding. Swan took a principal role investigating the incident, relying upon the help of Chetzamoka. Later, on March 18, he helped bury Swell. With the approval of Swell's brother Peter, he repainted Swell's *tomanawos* board and helped Peter place it as the base of the burial monument. Swan observed in his journal that Swell had never divulged the meaning or identity of the characters on his board, but before he left the gravesite, he sketched the monument and the board at its base (pages 78 & 79).[28]

Two days later Swan took time to complete an interior view of the lodge of Colchote, a leading man among the Makah (page 81). Swan commented in his journal that although the Makah did not generally inscribe their history in carvings, the designs on the columns that supported the roof of Colchote's lodge seemed to be such memorials. Swan regretted that he lacked a good translator who could provide detailed information about the figures, but he asked Russian Jim, who spoke the Chinook jargon "indifferently," to interpret

25 *Almost Out of the World*, 78-79.

26 *Indians of Cape Flattery*, 9. Swan wrote that "Capt John or Claplanhoo has requested me to make him some Tomanawos paintings. He said I want them made to represent something that the Indians never saw." James G. Swan, "Bound autograph manuscript journal and memorandum book: 1861-71," box 10, folder 191, *Franz R. and Kathryn M. Stenzel Collection of Western Art*, 95-96.

27 *Captured Heritage*, 14–47; *Swan Among the Indians*, 78–82.

28 Swan, *Almost Out of the World*, 100–104; Swan's description of repainting Swell's *tomanawos* board and helping to bury him appears in his "Bound autograph manuscript journal and memorandum book: 1861-71," 94.

what Colchote and his wife had to say. The leftmost column represented "Deeahks or Deeah," an ancestor who, Colchote claimed, was the first Makah to settle the area and for whom the Makah named the bay and surrounding countryside. The middle column depicted Klessakady or Sunrise. The head between his feet symbolized night, and the beam that his head supported was decorated with stars. According to Colchote, the statue might be said "to show the manner in which the sun, when rising, thrusts the stars away with his head and tramples the night under his feet." The final column represented Billaksakut'hl, "some fallen giant of antiquity like the colossus of Rhodes," through whose legs the largest canoes could pass. [29]

Swan reported that Colchote, who carved the final column himself, had hired a Nitinaht artist from Vancouver Island to shape Deeah and employed Dick, one of Peter's slaves, to carve Klessakady. After Colchote's death, Swan asked Dick about the column's meaning, and was amused when the artist reported that

he had no other idea than to cut some posts to look like men, and that so far as the head between the feet of Klessakady was concerned, it simply meant nothing; but there happened to be a big knot in the wood, which made it difficult to carve, so he made a head of it; and after it was done, Kalchote painted it and set it up in his lodge with the other two, and gave them names, and invented the allegory himself. He explained himself further by remarking that he would carve me a figure if I would like, and that I could make any meaning to it I chose.

Swan closed his discussion with the observation that most of the Makah dismissed Colchote's interpretation as his own invention and regarded the pole as "only Dick's work, which he did, with no particular object in view."[30]

During the summer and fall of 1861, Swan traveled frequently to Cape Flattery and beyond. In July, he visited the Quileute Indians, who lived south of the Makah along the Pacific coast, sketching the entrance to their harbor and making a rough, preliminary sketch of their village (pages 90 & 154). It may have been on this trip that he made several sketches of the rocky shores around Cape Flattery, including the Fuca Pillar at the extreme northwest corner of the contiguous United States (pages 91, 92, 94). He also sketched the British steamer *Hecate* after it ran aground just inside the Cape that summer (page 93).[31]

In October 1861 the Indian office hired Swan to conduct a census of the Makah, a sensitive undertaking which tested Swan's considerable diplomatic skills. He visited every lodge in all five of the Makah villages: Neah Bay, Baadah, Wayatch, Tsoo-yess, and Ozette. Perhaps it was Swan's success in persuading the Makah to allow the United States to count them that led the Indian office to offer him, in summer of 1862, the position of teacher at Neah Bay, a post he filled for more than four years. Ivan Doig wryly observes that as the school house was the westernmost building at Neah Bay, when Swan settled in, "he made himself in that moment the westernmost frontiersman in the continental United States."[32]

As he taught, Swan continued to research Makah culture and to send artifacts as well as natural history specimens to the Smithsonian, but the Stenzel collection contains relatively

---

29 Swan, "Bound autograph manuscript journal and memorandum book: 1861-71," 91-92; *Indians of Cape Flattery*, 58-59; Also see Swan's handwritten notes on the back of the drawing.

30 *Indians of Cape Flattery*, 59.

31 *Almost Out of the World*, 38-41.

32 Information about Swan's censuses of 1861, 1863, 1864, and 1865 appears in Swan, "Bound autograph manuscript journal and memorandum book: 1861-71," 39-66 & [137-153], [160-73], and [180-189]; *Winter Brothers*, 75.

few pictures from this period. He painted scenes from the Tsi-ahk or medicine dance of the Makah in 1861 and again in 1863 (pages 82–85) as well as a watercolor of the settlement at Baada in 1862 (page 88). An 1865 watercolor of an unidentified house seems likely to be from Neah Bay (page 89).[33]

In April of 1865 Swan submitted the manuscript for *The Indians of Cape Flattery* to Spencer Baird, Assistant Secretary of the Smithsonian Institution. The book, published by the Smithsonian in 1869, reflects the halting, gradual emergence of ethnography as a discipline in America. Whereas *The Northwest Coast* had been autobiographical in character, with Swan's observations about Indians interspersed with the narrative of his time at Shoalwater Bay, *The Indians of Cape Flattery* focused on the Makah in systematic fashion. Informed by his personal experience and extensive if untutored reading about Indians, Swan's descriptive passages are the book's greatest strength. The first detailed study of the Makah, it remains today a valuable account of their life before the great transformations that followed the federal government's decisions at the end of the century to restrict sealing and whaling and to compel all Makah children to attend federal schools.[34]

Eighteen months after submitting his manuscript, in October 1866, Swan resigned his teaching position and traveled to Boston to collect an inheritance. After visiting family, he went to Washington, D. C., to explore prospects for government service in the Northwest, particularly with the Indian bureau or the Smithsonian. When nothing developed in either branch, he returned to Port Townsend in July 1867. For the first time, he entered aggressively into the commercial and civic life of the frontier port. Perhaps the publication of his monograph had satisfied his curiosity about Indian culture. Perhaps the failure of officials in Washington to offer him a salaried position of responsibility in Indian affairs rankled him, leaving him unwilling to act as an informal assistant. Perhaps, as he neared his fiftieth birthday, financial concerns weighed more heavily. Whatever the cause, for the next six years Swan spent more time exploring ways to promote his and Port Townsend's commercial success than investigating Indian life.

In the fall of 1868 Swan opened a correspondence with Thomas Canfield, a director of the Northern Pacific Rail Road company. Chartered in 1864, the Northern Pacific planned to build a transcontinental road from Duluth to Puget Sound. Swan persuaded Canfield that he could provide invaluable information about the various harbors on the Sound to assist the company's selection of a terminus. His principal report was published in 1870 in a privately circulated pamphlet entitled *Northern Pacific Railroad; Partial Report of the Board of Directors of a Portion of a Reconnaissance Made in the Summer of 1869*. Swan's uncritical and unrealistic enthusiasm regarding Port Townsend undermined his credibility, and his employment ended when the Panic of 1873 toppled the company's original management. The Stenzel collection contains no drawings or watercolors of Port Townsend or Puget Sound from this time. As in the case of his time in California, it is uncertain whether Swan stopped making pictures or they have been lost.

As Swan tried to piece together a career, he did not altogether abandon his interest in collecting Indian and natural history artifacts. Continuing to correspond with Spencer Baird, he summarized his efforts to establish himself at Port

---

33 Ceremonies of November 1861 are described by Swan in his "Bound autograph manuscript journal and memorandum book: 1861-71," 77.

34 Ann M. Renker and Erna Gunther, "Makah" in *Handbook of North American Indians. Volume 7: The Northwest Coast*, ed. Wayne Suttles (Washington, 1990), 422-430.

Townsend. He had, he wrote Baird, "been appointed by the Governor as a notary public and Pilot Commissioner, and by the Supreme Court as United States Commissioner, and ... appointed myself as a commission merchant and ship broker." But he continued to struggle financially, observing wryly, "I reverse the saying that a prophet is without honor for I have the honors without the profit."[35] Other letters emphasized how much important material he could gather for the Smithsonian, if only it would provide the funds to subsidize his collecting. On his own account, Swan made his first visit to Alaska in the fall of 1869, during which trip he sketched Fort Simpson, the Hudson's Bay Company trading post in British Columbia, and the United States military post at Tongass, Alaska (pages 96 & 97).[36]

Swan's fascination with Indian culture blossomed anew in May 1873 when a group of Haida Indians who were visiting Port Townsend sought him to trade artifacts. Swan's reputation as a collector who would pay, with cash or goods, for Indian tools and art work had preceded him among the Haida, and as it had in the past, Swan's sincere interest in learning about the Indians laid a foundation for enduring friendships. The Haida, from the village of Klue (also called Tanu) in the Queen Charlotte Islands, spent days at Swan's office. Kitkune, a leading man, and three others allowed Swan to sketch the extensive tattoos with which the Haida decorated themselves. Swan persuaded Geneskelos, a brother of Kitkune, to make some drawings of his own, a reprise of Swan's earlier work with Yellicom and Kitchen-sum among the Makah and a fore-shadowing of future collaboration with another Haida artist,

Johnny Kit Elswa. At least two of the drawing made by Geneskelos are now at the Smithsonian Institution.[37]

Swan quickly wrote a brief, illustrated paper on Haida tattoos that the Smithsonian published the next year, *The Haidah Indians of the Queen Charlottes Islands, British Columbia. With a Brief Description of Their Carvings, Tattoo designs, etc.* Swan remained interested in the subject and a decade later, after he traveled to the Queen Charlotte Islands, he prepared another essay to be included in Garrick Mallery's *Pictographs of the North American Indians.* The sketches of tattoos reproduced here are, for the most part, undated, but it seems likely that two sheets of rough sketches made on paper torn from a business ledger (pages 100 & 101) are from Swan's May 1873 encounter; they closely resemble drawings reproduced in his 1874 study (page 102). The sketch on page 103, dated 1879, appears to be a preliminary drawing later reproduced in Mallery's study, while pages 104 and 105 reproduce additional rough sketches made in January, 1881. The National Anthropological Archives at the Smithsonian holds nine manuscript pages and one proof sheet of drawings for *The Haidah Indians* as well as three drawings by Swan in its Mallery collection of material related to sign language and pictography.[38]

The Haida visit revitalized Swan's enthusiasm for exploring Indian history and culture. He badgered Spencer Baird about the grand opportunities the Smithsonian would

---

35 *Winter Brothers,* 135.
36 *Captured Heritage,* 17-18.

37 *Winter Brothers,* 147; John Ewers, "The Emergence of the Named Indian Artist in the American West," *American Indian Art Magazine* (1981), Vol. 6, no. 2, 57.
38 James G. Swan, *Haidah Indians of the Queen Charlottes Islands, British Columbia. With a Brief Description of their Carvings, Tattoo Designs, etc,* (Washington, D. C., 1874); Garrick Mallery, *Pictographs of the North American Indians; A Preliminary Paper* (Washington, D. C., 1886); The National Anthropological Archives at the Smithsonian Institution have nine manuscript pages and some proof sheets from Swan, stored as NAA Ms 3987. The Mallery papers at the Smithsonian are NAA Ms 2372.

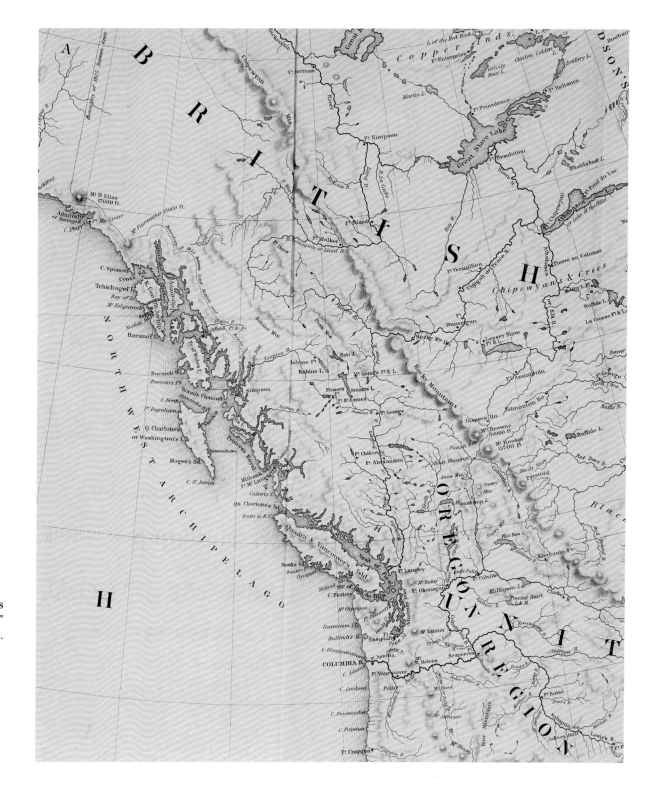

Detail from "Map of the middle and western portions
of North America . . . by Robert Greenhow."
From his *The History of Oregon and California . . .* (1844).

miss if it did not provide money for him to acquire artifacts. Baird, short of funds, humored Swan as best he could, thanked him for his past gifts, and expressed the hope that the government could, sometime soon, subsidize him to make an extensive collecting trip. Meanwhile, Swan continued to build a small museum collection in his Port Townsend office. Photographs show him surrounded by Indian tools and art. On November 20, 1873, Dr. Franz Steindachner, director of the Imperial Zoological Museum in Vienna visited, expressed interest in translating *The Indians of Cape Flattery* into German, and proposed to buy many of the specimens in Swan's office. Swan completed the sale and wrote Baird that if the Smithsonian was not interested, he would work with other parties. Baird answered that Congress would soon authorize an extensive ethnographic exhibit at the Centennial Exposition and that he wanted Swan to lead the effort to collect Northwestern material.[39]

When another inheritance drew Swan east to visit family in early 1874, he met with Baird to discuss the centennial exhibition. Congressional delay tempered their mutual enthusiasm and reduced the scale of their undertaking, but Swan eventually received a short-term, salaried appointment and a budget of $10,000. In June 1875 he sailed to British Columbia and Alaska aboard the United States revenue cutter *Oliver Wolcott*. During the trip, he visited Nanaimo, Fort Simpson, Fort Wrangall, Sitka, Koutznow (also known as Kootznahoo), Kake, Klawak, Howkan, Kasaan, Shigan, and Klinkwan. He purchased numerous Tlingit, Tsimshian, Bella Bella, and Kaigani Haidi artifacts from Alaska to join strong collections of Makah and Nootka material he had collected from either side of the Strait of Juan de Fuca. He could not visit the Queen Charlotte Islands, but he commissioned Geneskelos to paint an Indian canoe for the exhibit. When the exposition opened in Philadelphia on May 10, 1876, some 500 of Swan's pieces were exhibited. Regrettably, no drawings from the period exist in the Stenzel collection. Swan's report to the Bureau of Indian Affairs, first published in the annual report of the Commissioner of Indian Affairs, was reprinted in the Port Townsend *Argus* in September 1877 and later as an appendix to *The Report upon the Customs District, Public Service, and Resources of Alaska Territory* by William Gouverneur Morris, published by Congress in 1879.[40]

Swan's work in 1875 earned him Baird's loyal support, but following the fevered hunt for artifacts to display at the nation's centennial birthday party, Baird found Congress unwilling to provide the Smithsonian with money to continue collecting. After closing his accounts with the government, Swan spent most of 1876 and 1877 in Port Townsend and its immediate environs. In July 1878, his longtime friend Henry Webster, now collector of customs for Puget Sound, appointed Swan inspector at Neah Bay. Charles Willoughby, the agent at the Makah reservation, welcomed Swan and offered him a role as interpreter at the agency. Swan worked at Neah Bay through August 1881, when a new collector of customs installed an associate as Swan's successor. During his second tenure among the Makah, Swan painted watercolors of local plants (page 51 & 52) and of the light house on Tatoosh Island off Cape Flattery (page 115). He made another sketch of the Fuca Pillar (page 110), and it seems probable that an undated drawing that depicts his home at Neah Bay (page 113) comes from this period. In his final months at Neah Bay, Swan used a

---

39 *Captured Heritage*, 17-19.

40 *Ibid.*, 27-30; Ewers, "The Emergence of the named Indian Artist in the American West," *American Indian Art Magazine* (1981), Vol. 6, no. 2, 58.

small appropriation from Baird to buy a fine Clayoquot sealing club for the Smithsonian. His detailed drawing of the club, annotated with his description of the images on it, is reproduced on page 107.[41]

As Swan returned to Port Townsend in the late summer of 1881, a variety of American and German museums had begun to collect aggressively along the Northwest Coast. Through its close relationship with Swan, the Smithsonian had enjoyed a virtual monopoly in the field for twenty years. Now, as Spencer Baird grew concerned about competition, he sought funds to underwrite more extensive collecting by his principal agent in the Northwest. He turned to two sources that had recently become available to him. In addition to his duties at the Smithsonian, Baird now served as chairman of the United States Fish Commission, in which capacity he had prepared an award-winning exhibition of American aboriginal fishing practices for the 1880 Berlin Fisheries Exhibition. In 1882 he received from Congress a large appropriation to prepare an exhibition for the 1883 International Fisheries Exposition in London. In September of 1882 he hired Swan to work as "Assistant and Collector for the Fish Commission," and instructed him to emphasize specimens relating to whaling, sealing, and fishing but also to acquire as well "all you can of other illustrations of the Ethnology and Archaeology of the North West."[42]

To support Swan's collecting further, Baird assigned to him funds appropriated for John Wesley Powell's Bureau of Ethnology. Although Powell exercised considerable independence, the bureau had been transferred from the Interior Department to the Smithsonian, and Baird insisted that a por-

tion of its budget be devoted to collecting in the Northwest, an area in which Powell had no contacts and in which Baird regarded Swan as most qualified. On January 31, 1883, Baird wrote to Swan that the Smithsonian could underwrite an expedition to the Queen Charlotte Islands during the coming summer.[43]

Swan had wanted to visit the Queen Charlotte Islands, or *Haida Gwaii*, since Kitkune's party visited him in 1873. Over the decade, he had continued to entertain Haida visitors to Port Townsend, even allowing one silversmith, Ellswarsh, to work in his office making jewelry for several weeks.[44] Early in the spring of 1883, Swan hired another young Haida to serve as a guide, interpreter, and general assistant. Johnny Kit Elswa, "a working jeweler skilled in making silver bracelets, ear rings, and charms, and a good carver in wood and stone," hailed from "the Klue or Cumeshewa district on the eastern coast of Moresby Island." He spoke English fluently, and drew in the Haida style. Swan praised him as "one of the most intelligent, faithful and reliable" Indians he had ever met, and assured Baird that Kit Elswa would provide greater entrée than any other collector had ever enjoyed among the Haida.[45]

Kit Elswa remains an obscure figure in Northwestern history. Swan's description of his origins is ambiguous, for Klue and Cumshewa were distinct villages. Perhaps Swan was uncertain which village had been Kit Elswa's home. Perhaps

41 *Winter Brothers*, 164–176.
42 *Captured Heritage*, 34–39.

43 *Ibid.*, 38–40.
44 *Winter Brothers*, 223–224.
45 *Captured Heritage*,40; James Swan, "Synopsis of a report of work done in the Queen Charlotte Islands British Columbia, during the summer of 1883, under instructions from Professor Spencer F. Baird." ADS sent to Spencer Baird, Jan 16, 1884, box 10, folder 195, *Franz R. and Kathryn M. Stenzel Collection of Western Art.* This report was published as "Report on Exploration and Collections in the Queen Charlotte Islands, British Columbia," in *Annual Report of the Board of Regents of the Smithsonian Institution...for the year 1884,* (Washington, D. C., 1885), 137-146.

Kit Elswa had lived in both, for in the last half of the nine-teenth century, confronted by an extraordinary demographic disaster, entire Haida villages relocated themselves. Various epidemic diseases reduced the population of the Queen Charlotte Islands from over 6,000 people in 1836 to fewer than a thousand by 1890.[46] Many towns were devastated, and survivors took refuge in a handful of sites. In the early nineteenth century Klue and Cumshewa were two of some eighteen principal villages located throughout the archipelago. By 1900 most Haida lived in two towns on the Graham Island, the principal northern island of the Queen Charlotte chain. Masset was located on Graham's northern shore, while Skidegate was in the south, across a narrow strait from Moresby Island, the major southern island. During his trip Swan would visit numerous deserted towns as well as several villages which were abandoned shortly afterwards.[47]

Kit Elswa's history after his trip with Swan is as obscure as his origins. He may be the Johnny Swan to whom Franz Boas refers in his 1888 diary and in his 1895 publication of Northwestern Indian legends, *Indianische Sagen von der Nord-Pacifischen Küste Amerikas*.[48] As late as 1889 Swan wrote to alert the Smithsonian that through the assistance of Kit Elswa he could obtain valuable Bella Coola material from British Columbia, but references to Kit Elswa after 1889 have not been found.[49] In 1897 the collector C. F. Newcombe met Josephine Elswa, certainly at one time Johnny's wife but perhaps then his widow, at Skidegate.[50]

Despite the difficulty of establishing Kit Elswa's personal history, our knowledge of Haida customs allow us to make some tentative assertions about him. Haida carvers were generally men of high social standing who had received extensive formal training and who worked within well defined artistic traditions.[51] Artists among the Haida derived their importance from the social role of the totem poles and crests they created; their work "proclaimed the rank and social affiliation of a man, his wife, or a deceased relative." Creating such art was, in the words of Bill Holm, "both a responsibility of nobility and an affirmation of that nobility."[52] As in the case of Chetzamoka and Swell, Swan had befriended a man who could instruct him in the ways of the Haida and who probably enjoyed sufficient prestige to open doors that would otherwise be closed to an outsider.

Swan and Kit Elswa left Port Townsend on May 29. They stopped in Victoria to board the Hudson's Bay Company steamer *Otter* and arrived at Masset, on the north end of Graham Island, on June 26. Swan distinguished Masset, the site of a Hudson's Bay Company post, from the Haida village, Uttewas. He estimated that in Uttewas there were about 65 houses, some of which were in ruins. "Nearly every house has a carved column erected in front covered with Heraldic or totemic designs of the family residing within."[53] For the next six

---

46 Margaret B. Blackman, "Haida: Traditional Culture," *Handbook of North American Indians; Volume 7: Northwest Coast*, 257-258.

47 George F. MacDonald, *Chiefs of the Sea and Sky: Haida Heritage Sites of the Queen Charlotte Islands*, (Vancouver, 1989) provides a useful overview of Haida village histories.

48 Franz Boas, *Indianische Sagen von der Nord-Pacifischen Küste Amerikas*, (Berlin, 1895). See the English translation, *Indian myths & legends from the North Pacific Coast of America*, ed. Randy Bouchard and Dorothy Kennedy; translated by Dietrich Bertz (Vancouver, 2002), 597, 604, 608. Also see *The Ethnography of Franz Boas*, ed. Ronald P. Rohner, translated by Hedy Parker (Chicago, 1969), 90, 97.

49 *Captured Heritage*, 46.

50 *Ibid.*, 180.

51 Robin K. Wright, *Northern Haida Master Carvers*, (Seattle, 2001), 5.

52 Bill Holm, "Art," *Handbook of North American Indians; Volume 7: Northwest Coast*, 615.

weeks, Swan visited among the Haida at Uttewas and made short trips to the surrounding countryside (pages 117, 118, 119). In coming to Graham Island, Swan had deliberately traveled beyond the region with which Kit Elswa was most familiar and where he could be most helpful, but Swan had settled on a plan to explore the western coast of Graham Island, an imperfectly charted area which had never been canvassed by ethnographers or collectors. Only a few years earlier Canadian geologist George Dawson had given up surveying the region, suggesting that the only way to do so would be by canoe in summer. Now, at Masset, Swan sought a Haida guide who could escort him past North or Langara Island, around the northwest corner of Graham Island, and down the western coast while at the same time showing him the abandoned town sites. Only afterwards would he would visit Kit Elswa's country south of Skidegate.[54]

Swan secured the aid of a legendary figure, Albert Edward Edenshaw, referred to by Swan as "Edinso." Sometime around 1832, when he was about 22 years old, Albert Edenshaw became chief man of Kiusta, a village on the northwest coast of Graham Island. He gained renown as a canoe maker and for his elaborate work in copper and steel. In 1853 Edenshaw and most of Kiusta's surviving residents moved east to Kung, where he built a famous lodge known as "House that can hold a great crowd of people." Sometime around 1880, the villagers abandoned Kung and moved to Masset, where Swan met him. While at Masset, Swan also visited Albert's nephew Charles Edenshaw, who would soon be recognized as one of the great Haida artists. Charles worked in a wide variety of

James Swan and Johnny Kit Elswa, October 1883.

53 James Swan, "Synopsis of a report of work done in the Queen Charlotte Islands British Columbia...," 3.
54 *Winter Brothers*, 182–184.

media, and Swan purchased two ivory cane handles from him.[55]

On August 6, Swan and Kit Elswa left Masset in a Haida canoe commanded by Albert Edenshaw. The next day, as they passed Klatagewos or Pillar Rock, Swan made a rough sketch of it in his journal; a later version appears on page 120. That afternoon the party landed at Kiusta, where they stayed for a week, during which time Swan sketched Edenshaw's old house (page 121) and the village's "heraldic columns," one of which appears here on page 122. From Kiusta, Swan made a variety of day trips including one to the abandoned village of Yaku (which he renders as "Yakh" in the drawing reproduced on page 123) and another to North Island, where he sketched the burial house of a famous shaman (page 124) and an ancient column embedded in a spruce tree (page 125). At Kiusta, Johnny Kit Elswa began work on a series of drawings "illustrative of Indian legends."[56]

After leaving Kiusta on August 14, the party encountered foul weather and difficult tides which slowed their progress down the coast. They took refuge near Cape Knox, and Swan spent three days exploring up and down the shore. He was fascinated by the countryside, which he described as "thrown into various contorted and fantastic shapes by volcanic action. It presents a most remarkable formation." For once, nature overwhelmed Swan's skills as a draftsman. He remarked to Baird, "I regretted that I did not have a photo-

graphic apparatus with me to have taken a view of the scene which it is impossible otherwise to describe."[57]

Finally, after much discomfort and considerable apprehension when Edenshaw's canoe developed a crack in its hull, the party reached Skidegate on August 26. As Masset had become the principal northern village, drawing to it Haida refugees from many abandoned villages along the northern coast, Skidegate was in the process of becoming the main village for the southern Haida. Located on the northern side of the strait that separates Graham and Moresby Islands, it contained some thirty houses in the early 1880s and grew larger over the next few years. At Skidegate, Swan re-united with Ellswarsh, the silversmith he had befriended in Port Townsend years earlier. He spent eight days at the village, "making collections" and sketching houses and their poles (pages 126 & 127).[58]

On September 4, Ellswarsh accompanied Swan and Kit Elswa as they traveled to Skedans and Kit Elswa's home district of Cumshewa and Klue. In comparison to Masset and Skidegate, which were strongly influenced by missionaries, villages along the eastern coast of Moresby Island and on the other southern islands had resisted abandoning their customs. At Klue, on Laskeek Bay, Swan found "the most interesting collection of columns, both heraldic and mortuary, and more monuments for the dead than I had seen in any other village."[59] He learned that Kitkune, the chief who visited him in Port Townsend in 1873, had died and been succeeded by a nephew who married his widow and assumed his name. The new chief welcomed Swan as a friend and took him to his

55 For information about the Edenshaws see George F. MacDonald, "The Haida: Children of Eagle and Raven," an electronic publication of the Canadian Museum of Civilization Corporation at http://www.civilization.ca/aborig/haida/haindexe.html#menu (1998, 2001) as well as MacDonald's *Haida Art* (Seattle, 1996). Doig relates the story behind Swan's purchase of the canes in *Winter Brothers*, 190-191 and 195.

56 James Swan, "Synopsis of a report of work done in the Queen Charlotte Islands British Columbia…," 6-7.

57 *Ibid.*, 7

58 *Ibid.*, 8 and *Winter Brothers*, 208-211 and 215-223.

59 James Swan, "Synopsis of a report of work done in the Queen Charlotte Islands British Columbia…," 9.

newly built house where, in a few weeks, he would throw what became one of the last traditional potlatches celebrated among the Haida.[60] To validate his ascension to leadership, Kitkune had constructed the new home,

of large dimensions, built after the ancient style. In this house will he hold the most extensive ceremonies that have taken place for many years, consisting of the Tamanawos or secret performances, then the public tattooing of persons of all ages and sexes, then the masquerade dances, and the distribution of presents, when several thousand dollars worth of blankets, calico clothing, and provisions will be given away, and the whole interspersed with feasts at different houses in the village. The occasion of this is the erection of one or more huge columns elaborately carved with totemic devices to show the wealth and importance of the chief in front of whose house the columns will be erected.[61]

Swan regretted that he would not be able to attend, "as it is probable that it will be the last grand display of the kind that will take place, the influence of the missionaries being directed to suppressing these ancient customs." Swan prophesied accurately. Within a few years the town was abandoned; its inhabitants relocated to Skidegate. Swan's hurried sketch of Kitkune's house (page 128) captured the epic scale of the poles at Klue.[62]

Swan and Kit Elswa returned to Victoria on September 27. They eventually shipped twenty-nine crates of Indian artifacts and fish to Baird. It is likely that Swan also sent a small collection of drawings from the expedition. A set of undated drawings that the Smithsonian calls "Manuscript Proofsheets: Swan, James G., Artist" includes six detailed depictions of Haida totem poles accompanied by extensive manuscript notes explaining the iconography of the poles. Although the captions do not reveal the village locations of the poles, the style of drawing and annotation closely resemble the drawings reproduced here on pages 117 through 129.[63] Although the Smithsonian catalog reports that no provenance information can be found, another small collection of nine rough drawings in pen, ink, and graphite almost certainly records the first portion of Swan's 1883 voyage. Primarily of scenes around Fort Simpson, they resemble the undated sketch of an Indian boy in a boat on Barclay Sound, Vancouver Island, reproduced here as page 159.[64]

Swan did not send to the Smithsonian the set of drawings made by Johnny Kit Elswa. Instead, in August 1884 he reproduced five of them in an article that he wrote for *West*

---

60 *Captured Heritage*, 43.

61 James Swan, "Synopsis of a report of work done in the Queen Charlotte Islands British Columbia…,"9.

62 *Ibid.*, 9

63 James G. Swan, *Manuscript Proofsheets*, National Anthropological Archives, Smithsonian Institution, six graphite on paper drawings on cardboard mounts. Individual items include: *Totem pole, slate: with beaver, frog, bear, and crayfish figures (Front View); carved by Haida, Queen Charlotte Islands, British Columbia* (NAA Inv. 08541901) *Totem pole, slate: with old woman figure wearing claw hat, eagle and bear figure (side view); carved by Haida, Queen Charlotte Islands, British Columbia* (NAA Inv. 08541902) *Totem pole, slate: with old woman figure wearing claw hat, eagle and bear figure (front view); carved by Haida, Queen Charlotte Islands, British Columbia* (NAA Inv. 08541903) *Totem pole, slate: with young bear, wolf, and sea lion figures (front view); Carved by Haida, Queen Charlotte Islands, British Columbia* (NAA Inv. 08541904) *Totem pole, 4, slate: with carved effigy human and animal Figures (front and side views); carved by Haida, Queen Charlotte Islands, British Columbia* (NAA Inv. 08542000) *Totem pole, 4,slate: with carved effigy human and animal figures (front and side views); carved by Haida, Queen Charlotte Islands, British Columbia* (NAA Inv. 08542100)

64 "View of Fort Simpson (British Columbia), and Indians ca. 1880-83," Local Number: OPPS Neg 45,604 c—f. National Anthropological Archives, Smithsonian Institution. The seven pages of pen, brown ink and graphite drawings are attributed to Swan on the basis of handwritten (printed) captions and subject matter. "The drawings were found in USNM collection, without catalog cards or accession numbers."

Shore, an illustrated monthly published in Portland. The five originals, plus six other drawings by Kit Elswa, are part of the Stenzel collection, reproduced here as pages 133 through 143. As when he published Yellicom's drawing of the Makah Thunderbird, Swan took care in his article to explicate the legendary figures of Haida art. Two of the drawings he reproduced concerned Raven, the shape-shifting trickster whom the Haida credited with creating the world but who also caused continual mischief. "Raven (Hooyeh) in Whale (Koone)," (page 133) depicts the Haida explanation for dead whales washing ashore. Raven, they said, had gone to sea and been swallowed by a whale. To free himself, he changed shape, causing severe pain in the whale's belly. Frantic with pain, the whale rushed ashore, where the invisible Hooyeh quietly walked out and prepared for another adventure.[65]

Page 134, "Hooyeh the Raven. Houskana the fisherman," depicts another account of Raven as troublemaker. As before, the tale begins with Raven descending into the ocean, this time to frustrate the efforts of Houskana, the fisherman. Raven tangled his lines, stole his bait, and ate the fish off his hook. Houskana, tired of Raven's antics, used a magic hook from which Raven could not free himself. Raven resisted capture, pressing his feet and wings against the bottom of the fisherman's canoe, but Houskana was stronger. He pulled Raven's beak off, seized him, and took him ashore. Trying to escape discovery, Raven changed into human shape and covered his face so that Houskana could see only his eyes. Determined to find out who had caused him such trouble, the fisherman took a handful of filth and rubbed it into Raven's eyes, at which point he emerged. Raven was so angry that, ever since, he and

his friends the crows have persecuted fishermen "by soiling their canoes with their filthy droppings and eating all their fish."[66]

Raven was not the only powerful shape-shifter in Haida mythology. Page 135 depicts "Skana, the killer (orca)," a dangerous being from the underwater world, who could appear as a man or a killer whale. The image here portrays the spirit's double nature, depicting a man inside an orca. Page 136 presents Raven and Skana together, battling to possess a salmon.[67]

The Haida version of "The man in the moon" appears on page 137. According to Swan, when the moon, Koong, discovered the man, Eethlinga, about to dip his bucket into a brook, "it sent down its arms or rays and grabbed the man, who, to save himself, seized hold of a big salal bush, but the moon being more powerful took man and bucket and bush up to itself, where they have ever since lived and can be seen every full moon when the weather is clear."[68] The weather itself was a subject for Haida story tellers and page 138, "T'kul or cirrus clouds," depicts T'kul, the wind spirit, in the center of the composition. To either side

are his feet…above are the wings, and side are the different winds, each designated by an eye, and represented by the patches of cirrus clouds. When T'kul determines which wind is to blow, he gives the word and the other winds retire. The change in the weather is usually followed by rain, which is indicated in the tears which stream from the eyes of T'kul.[69]

Kit Elswa's other drawings depict animals that fre-

---

65 James G. Swan, "The Carvings and Heraldic Paintings of the Haida Indians," *The West Shore*, (Portland, Oregon) Vol. 10, no. 8 (August, 1884), 250.

66 *Ibid.,* 253.
67 *Ibid.,* 250.
68 *Ibid.,* 253.
69 *Ibid.,* 250.

quently appeared as heralds or totems on family crests or poles. Hooyeh, the Raven; Skulpin Kul and Kahalta, fish spirits; Wasko, a mythological mix of bear and killer whale; and Koot, the sparrow hawk (pages 139 through 143).

Drawing in ink on paper as Kit Elswa did was a recent innovation among the Haida. Haida artists had carved images in wood, stone, and metal for generations, serving the interests of their patrons and receiving a variety of traditional social and economic rewards. The appearance of European traders and settlers offered new patrons and new rewards, and, as Victoria Wyatt has discussed, Indian artists throughout the Northwest Coast responded by adapting traditional themes and practices to new media that European customers preferred, such as argillite or paper. The formline tradition that defined the decoration of Northwest Coast crests, boxes, and house boards was, Bill Holm observes, particularly easy to transfer to paper, and George F. MacDonald, who seems unaware of Kit Elswa, points out that Haida artists Charles Edenshaw, John Robson, Tom Price, and John Cross all began to experiment with painting on paper sometime in the 1880s. Edenshaw, the carver from whom Swan purchased an elegant pair of cane handles at Masset in 1883, made at least eight colored pencil drawings in 1897; they are now at the American Museum of Natural History. A few years later, museum collector C. F. Newcombe commissioned Robson (Edenshaw's step-father and already famous as a carver) to paint a set of crests for the Field Museum in Chicago. Although Kit Elswa may not have been the first to make the transition to drawing and painting on paper, the images he made for Swan are among the earliest known examples of such work. [70]

Regrettably, Swan did not complete a major, illustrated

report on his trip to the Queen Charlotte Islands. A ten-page letter to Baird, prepared in January 1884, was published without illustration in the Smithsonian's *Annual Report of the Board of Regents* for 1885, but Swan never produced the equivalent of his *Northwest Coast* or *The Indians of Cape Flattery*.[71] The most complete use of his research on the Queen Charlotte Islands was made by Albert Niblack, whose *The Coast Indians of Southern Alaska and Northern British Columbia* described many of the artifacts Swan collected and reproduced the five Kit Elswa drawings that had appeared in *The West Shore*.[72] Swan's age, sixty-five, probably contributed to his not preparing a scholarly work, as did Baird's death in 1887. With his patron's passing, Swan found that a new generation of Smithsonian staff generally ignored him. Niblack was an exception, but as a naval officer, he was not particularly well placed to assist Swan.

Swan did garner considerable local attention upon his return to Victoria and Port Townsend. He addressed the Parliament of the Province of British Columbia on January 26, just ten days after submitting his report to Baird. That spring he became the Kingdom of Hawaii's consul in Port Townsend.

Northwest Coast Indian Art (New Haven, 1984), 52; Wyatt extends her discussion and interpretation in "Ethnic Identity" and Active Choice: Foundations of Indian Strength in Southeast Alaska, 1867-1912," Ph. D. thesis, Yale University History Dept., 1985. Wright, *Northern Haida Master Carvers* reproduces eight of Charles Edenshaw's colored pencil drawings of 1897 as well as two drawings by Robson. George MacDonald, "Haida Art: Flat Design," http://www.civilization.ca/aborig/haida/haaar02e.html.

71 James G. Swan, "Report on Exploration and Collections in the Queen Charlotte Islands, British Columbia," in *Annual Report of the Board of Regents of the Smithsonian Institution...for the year 1884*, (Washington, D. C., 1885), 137-146.

72 Albert Niblack, "The Coast Indians of Southern Alaska and Northern British Columbia," in A*nnual Report of the Board of Regents of the Smithsonian Institution...for the year ending June 30, 1888. Part II: Report of the United States National Museum* (Washington, 1890), 225-386.

70 Victoria Wyatt, *Shapes of their Thoughts: Reflections of Culture Contact in*

Over the summer of 1884, the Smithsonian granted him a commission to collect material for the Cotton Centennial Exposition in New Orleans, but Swan relied upon the many friendships he had made up and down the coast to gather artifacts without going beyond Neah Bay or Victoria.[73] Swan spent time writing a report on the Pacific "black cod," a fish from the coast of Graham Island that he appears to have been the first to describe, and the final dated work in the Stenzel collection is a watercolor drawing of the fish that he completed July 3, 1884 (page 145). At least some of the other drawings of fish found in the Stenzel collection date from this period (pages 146 through 151).[74]

Four years later, in 1888, Swan made a final trip east. He spent considerable time in his home town of Medford, and it is easy to imagine that he took pride in all he had accomplished since leaving Massachusetts forty years earlier. A few years later the State of Washington and Franz Boas hired him to collect material for the Chicago World's Fair of 1892, but shortly after he completed those tasks, the Panic of 1893 struck hard at the fortunes of Puget Sound in general and Port Townsend in particular. Swan had never saved much money, and his few investments in real estate were rendered worthless. Without any immediate family and with most of his friends in as much trouble as himself, his final years were difficult. On May 18, 1900, he passed away following a stroke.

One hundred years later, Swan's legacy opens multiple windows upon the American nineteenth century. The hundreds of artifacts he collected for the Smithsonian Institution remain, in the words of Douglas Cole, "a magnificent collec-

tion." From the time of Malaspina and Cook, European explorers and traders had gathered random examples of Northwest Coast Indian material culture, but Swan was the first person to collect in depth from Puget Sound to the Queen Charlotte Islands. He began twenty years before Franz Boas entered the field, and while he lacked Boas's linguistic and analytic skills, Swan gathered most of his material before 1885, when religious and government programs of forced acculturation contributed to rapid transformations of Indian life. His collections preserved a significant cultural record that permits us continually to reexamine and reconsider nineteenth-century Northwest Coast Indian history and culture.[75]

If the collections he made help us to understand Native American communities, Swan's drawings and watercolors reveal much about the role that images and image-making played in Victorian America. Neither innovative nor extraordinarily skilled as an artist, Swan was a talented draftsman whose work displays the visual vernacular of the mid-nineteenth-century frontier. As did so many of his contemporaries across the West, Swan found that drawing allowed him to expand upon ideas and capture information that he could not convey adequately with words alone. It would, however, be a mistake to think of his drawings as mere illustrations. They clearly meant a great deal to him, for he kept them till his death, carrying them with him from one remove to another. Like his diaries, the drawings were meditations upon his experiences. They surely held meanings for him that are difficult if not impossible for us to appreciate. Although we may not fully comprehend Swann's investment in his drawings, they remind

73 *Captured Heritage*, 45–46.

74 James G. Swan, "Report on Black Cod," *Bulletin of the United States Fish Commission* (Washington, D. C., 1885).

75 *Captured Heritage*, 47. The value of Swan's collections are reflected in the extensive discussion and reproduction of them in *Handbook of North American Indians; Volume 7: Northwest Coast.*

us that the art of image-making was not limited to the galleries and salons of eastern cities, but was also a part of the everyday life of many frontier residents. Like the artifacts he collected for the Smithsonian, Swan's concrete, descriptive drawings remind us that the past had a look and a shape as well as a language, that people saw as well as heard their history, that they lived among things as well as ideas. Joined to the many words in his four decades of diaries, Swan's pictures make the Olympic Peninsula of his time more accessible to both our imagination and our understanding.

If Swan was not innovative as an artist, he did explore new paths in his relationships with Native American artists. Swan showed no inclination to "play Indian" or to become a full-fledged member of an Indian community, but he clearly relished their company at a personal as well as an intellectual level. Whether picnicking with Chetzemoka and his wives at Hoff's mill, discussing the aurora borealis with Swell, chatting with the Makah artist David about the meaning of his sculpture, or sharing a leaky canoe with Haida elder Albert Edenshaw and his retinue, Swan enjoyed the friendship as well as the acquaintance of Indians. Artists garnered particular attention. While earlier students of Indian life had copied Indian designs and commented on their significance, Swan reached out to individual artists such as Kitchen-sum, David, Geneskelos, Ellswarsh, and Johnny Kit Elswa, soliciting them to draw and paint for him. His lifelong fascination with Indian iconography, with the links between pictures and stories, led him to encourage Indian artists to expand their repertoire to include works on paper in pencil, pen, and paint.

Swan's curiosity, enthusiasm, and willingness to share and trade drawings with Indian artists inspired their friendship and reflected his confidence in cultural collaboration. Much as Richard Henry Pratt and other army officers contributed to the development of Plains Indian ledger art and anthropologists J. Walter Fewkes and Edgar Hewitt assisted the growth of Pueblo easel painting, Swan, and the collectors who followed him, fostered the emergence of new forms of artistic expression among Northwest Coast Indians.[76] The new art was not Swan's creation, but he was clearly an important midwife assisting its birth. His exchanges with Indian artists capture what seems to have been for Swan the enduring attaction of the frontier: the opportunity to meet new people, contemplate new ideas, and share his knowledge with others. His pictures, like the stories in his diaries, remind us that amidst the violent conflict that marked so much of the nineteenth-century West, the frontier could also be a place of fluid creativity where people of different backgrounds came together to converse and grow. The pictures Swan made and collected challenge us to recognize that the geographic, political, and social boundaries that have emerged over time to separate Indian and white communities are neither permanent nor inevitable features of American history.

---

76 For recent scholarship on Plains ledger art, see *Plains Indian Drawings, 1865-1935: Pages from a Visual History*, ed. Janet Catherine Berlo (New York, 1996). Dorothy Dunn discusses J. Walter Fewkes and Edgar Hewitt in *American Indian Painting of the Southwest and Plains Areas* (Albuquerque, 1968), 190-194 and 198-203.

Botanical Watercolors

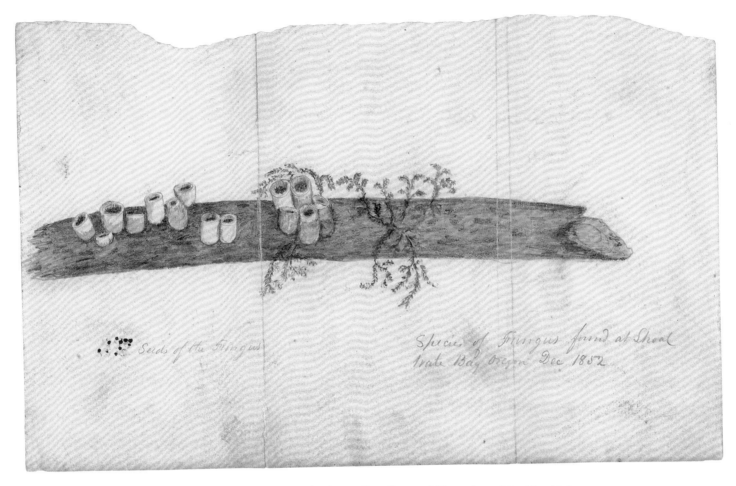

"Species of fungus found at Shoalwater Bay, Oregon." December 1852. 12 x 19.3 cm.

Right: "Raspberry." June 1854. 19.4 x 13.5 cm.

Opposite Left: "Arbutus Uva Ursi." 19.4 x 12.7 cm.

Opposite Right: "Clarkia." July 1854. 19.4 x 13 cm.

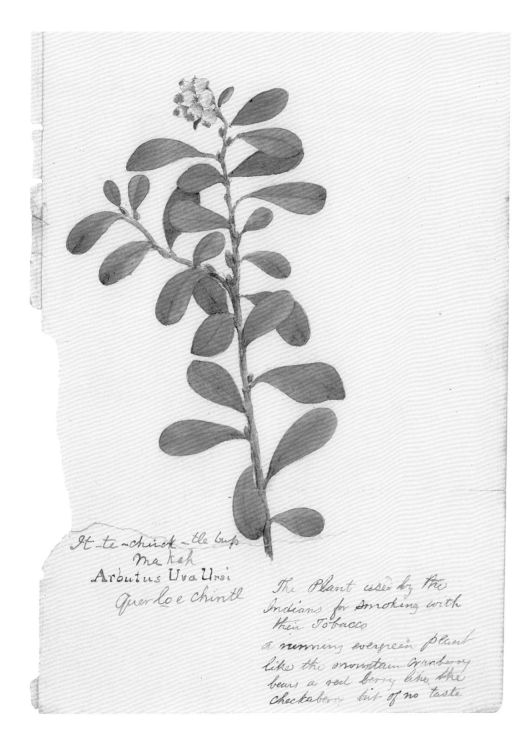

It-te-chuck-tle buch
Makah
Arbutus Uva Ursi
Querloe chintl

The Plant used by the
Indians for smoking with
their Tobacco
a running evergreen plant
like the mountain Cranberry
bears a red berry like the
checkaberry but of no taste

Epilopium
Po poke sa up

Sis-sis-litch
Makah

July 1854

Clarkia

Right: "Que uts quenin - Queniult." 20.4 x 14.4 cm.

Opposite Left: "Wild pea." June 1854. 20.4 x 14.1 cm.

Opposite Right: "Dicentra formosa." April 3. 20.4 x 13.9 cm.

Right: "Napea" July 1854. 20.4 x 14.2 cm.

Opposite Left: "Trillium." March 10. 20.4 x 13.9 cm.

Opposite Right: "Solomons seal." 20.4 x 13.7 cm.

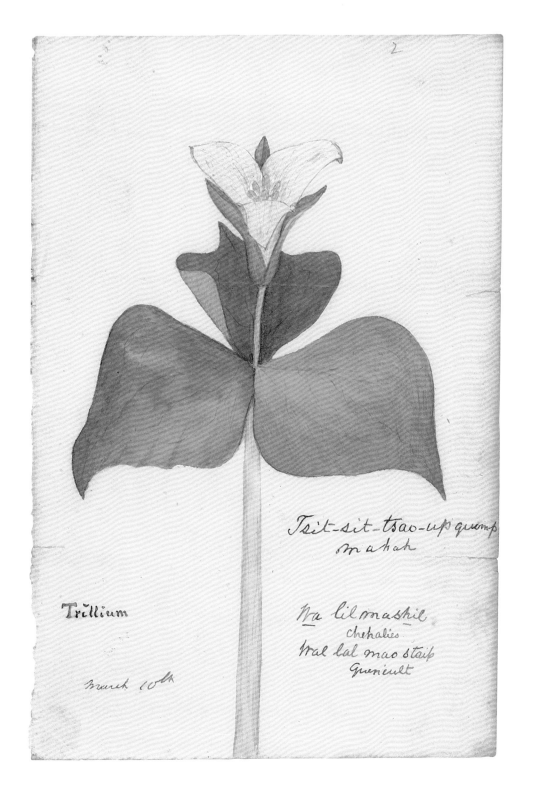

Tsit-sit-tsao-up quamp
makah

Trillium

Na lil mashil
chehalies
Wal bal mao staip
Guenieult

March 10th

Convallaria

Ha-uk-quoits-blossom
koo ake we muts-
makah   leaf

Solomons Seal

Shoal Water Bay
June 1854
Pa pay lute koko bup
Yellow lily

"Yellow lily. Shoalwater Bay." June 1854. 19.4 x 13 cm

Five plants from Neah Bay: Salmon berry, cammass (2), sallal, and konkiwhi. June 5, 1859. 19.1 x 24 cm.

Kau'la'uni

Salmon Berry
Rubus Spectabilis
Neah Bay W.T.
June 5ᵗ 1859

Cammass

qua-quanis-kook
mackah

Cammass
Cammassia
Esculenta

Sallal
Gaultheria Shallon
Neah Bay W.T.
June 5ᵗʰ 1859

Hull iar ka bupt - (makah)
The shrub used by the Indians to make the
disc or wheels used in playing the Gambling game
of La Hull

"Salmon Berry, Wake Robin, and species of cress found at Neeah Bay." [April 1861] 23 x 18 cm.

"Hull iar ka bupt - (Makah). The shrub used by the Indians to make the discs or wheels used in playing the gambling game of La Hull." 17 x 24 cm.

"Sallal." June 1873. 17.9 x 15.2 cm.

"Service berry." May 22, 1879. 25 x 17.8 cm.

Service berry. _Amelanchier Canadensis_ Ton.rG.
Neeah Bay W.T. May 22 1879   J G Swan, del.

Hil gʻaʻttle geah Haidah

Trillium Grandifolium
'Wake Robin'
May 1879. Neeah Bay W.T.
J G Swan.

"Trillium Grandifolium 'Wake Robin.'
May 1879. 35 x 25.2 cm.

Flower. 17.5 x 25.4 cm.

Early Drawings
from the Olympic Peninsula

"Queniult Village." [1854] 12 x 19.4 cm.

"Exterior of an Indian lodge." [ca. 1855] 12.2 x 19.5 cm.

"Treaty in the Chehalis between Gov. Stevens and 5 tribes Chinooks, Chehalis, Cowlitz, Queniult, & Satsops."
[February 1855] 12.7 x 19.5 cm.

"Interior of an Indian Lodge." [ca. 1855] 12.3 x 19.4 cm.

"Hoffs Old Mill, Chimakum." 1858 [but actually March, 1859] 18 x 23 cm.

Hoffs Old Mill Chimakum
now at mouth 1858

"The Tomanawos of the Clallam Indians, Port Townsend beach, Washington Territory." May 1, 1859. 18.1 x 23 cm.

The Tomanawos men as they appear when they first come out of their trance - The head dress is cedar bark dyed

"The Tomanawos men as they appear when the first come out of their trance - the head dress is cedar bark dyed." [May 1859 ?] 18.1 x 23 cm.

"Duke of York house. Jenny Lind distributing presents at Potlatch." [May 1859] 18.1 x 23 cm.

view on the Lummi Indian Reservation June 1 1859 view looking North

"View on the Lummi Indian Reservation. View looking North." June 1, 1859. 18.2 x 23 cm.

Clallam Bay or Cla cla wice M.S.
Capt Jacks residence. 1859.
The present site of the Hoko Cannery

J.G. Swan

"Clallam Bay or Cla cla wice. W.T. Capt. Jack's residence." 1859. 18.1 x 23 cm

"Port Townsend." 1859. 18 x 23 cm.

"Residence of Col. M. T. Simmons Skookum Bay Hammish Inlet, W.T." July 1859. 18 x 23 cm.

"Residence of Judge Sidney S. Ford, Chehalis W.T." [1859] 18 x 23 cm. n.d.

Wa addah Island

Baadah

"Waadah Island" and "Baadah Point, Neeah Bay." 1859. 17.6 x 50.6 cm.

Baadah Point Neeah Bay   JG Swan 1859

"Scene in a Makah Lodge, Neeah Bay." November 1859. 18.2 x 23 cm.

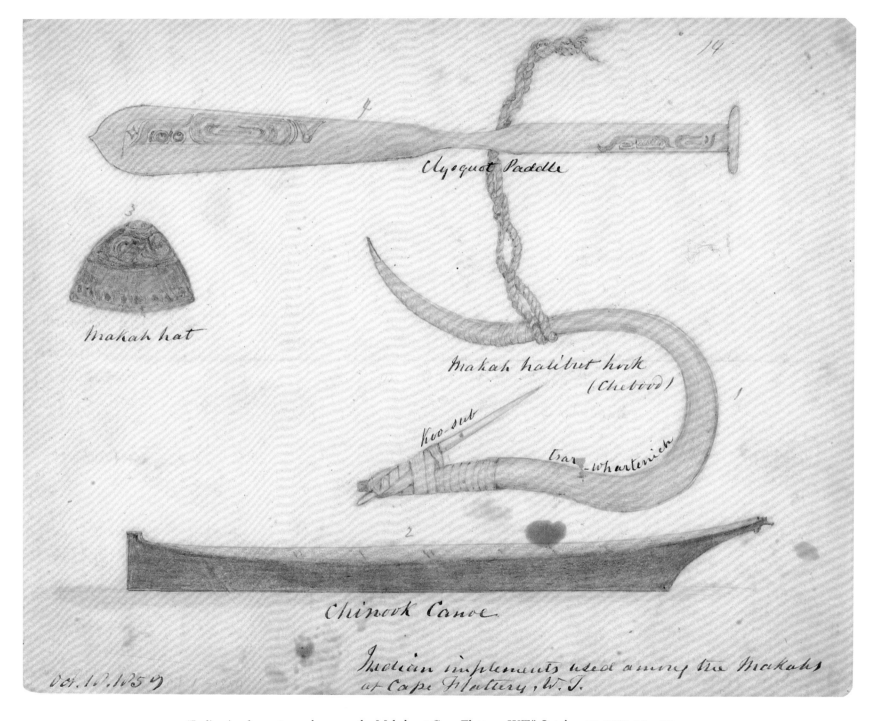

Clyoquot Paddle

Makah hat

Makah halibut hook
(Chebood)

Koo-sub

tsar-whartenich

Chinook Canoe

Oct. 18. 1859

Indian implements used among the Makahs at Cape Flattery, W.T.

"Indian implements used among the Makahs at Cape Flattery, W.T." October 18, 1859. 18 x 23 cm

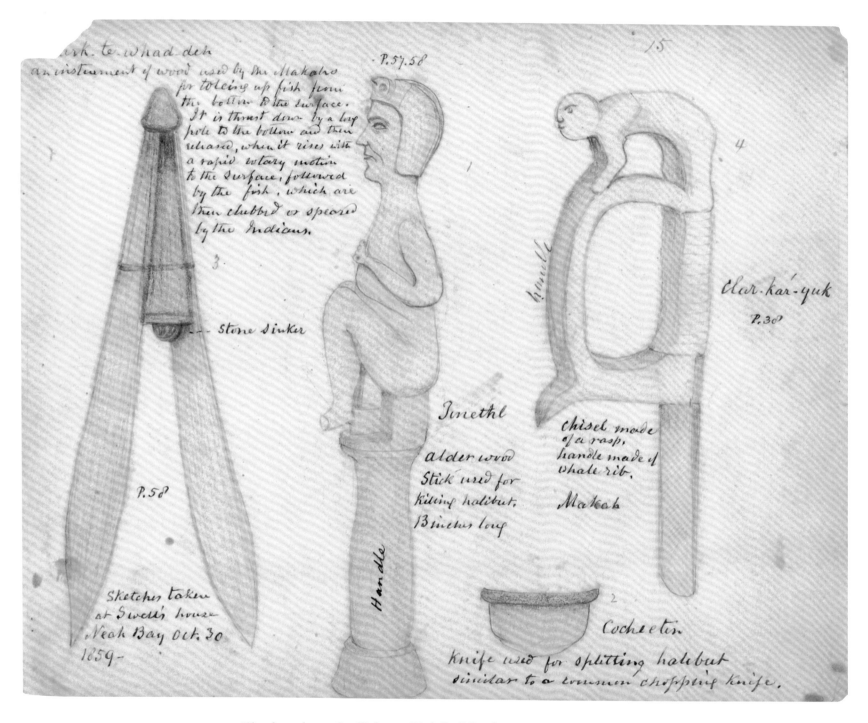

ark.te.whad.deh
an instrument of wood used by the Makahs
for toleing up fish from
the bottom to the surface.
It is thrust down by a long
pole to the bottom and then
released, when it rises with
a rapid rotary motion
to the surface, followed
by the fish, which are
then clubbed or speared
by the Indians.

P.57.58

15

3

Stone sinker

P.58

Sketches taken
at Swell's house
Neah Bay Oct. 30
1859.

Handle

Tinethl

alder wood
Stick used for
killing halibut.
13 inches long

handle

Chisel made
of a rasp,
handle made of
whale rib.

Makah

Clar.kar.yuk

P.30

4

Cocheetin

Knife used for splitting halibut
similar to a common chopping knife.

"Sketches taken at Swell's house, Neah Bay" October 30, 1859. 18.1 x 23 cm.

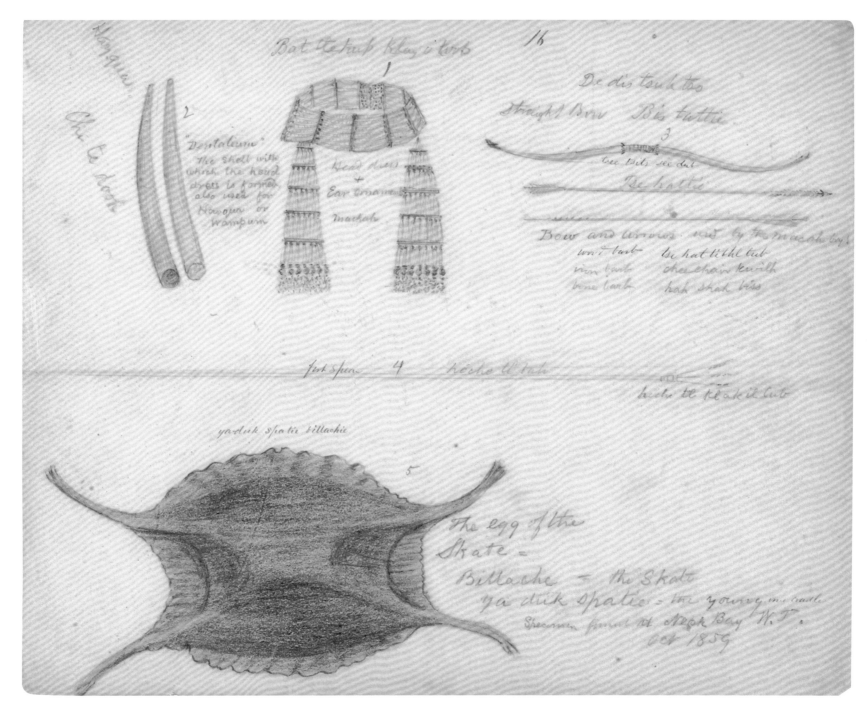

Headdress, bow and arrows, and skate. October 1859. 18.1 x 23 cm.

"Tomanawos masks used by the Mackah, Nootka & Clyoquot Indians. Wooden dish used by the Mackah Indians. Mackah basket." [1859 ?] 18.1 x 23 cm.

nov 6

Tomanawos or mediane board
Makah Indians
Neeah Bay W T

Nov 1859

"Tomanawos or medicine board. Makah Indians, Neah Bay, W.T." November 1859. 18.3 x 23 cm.

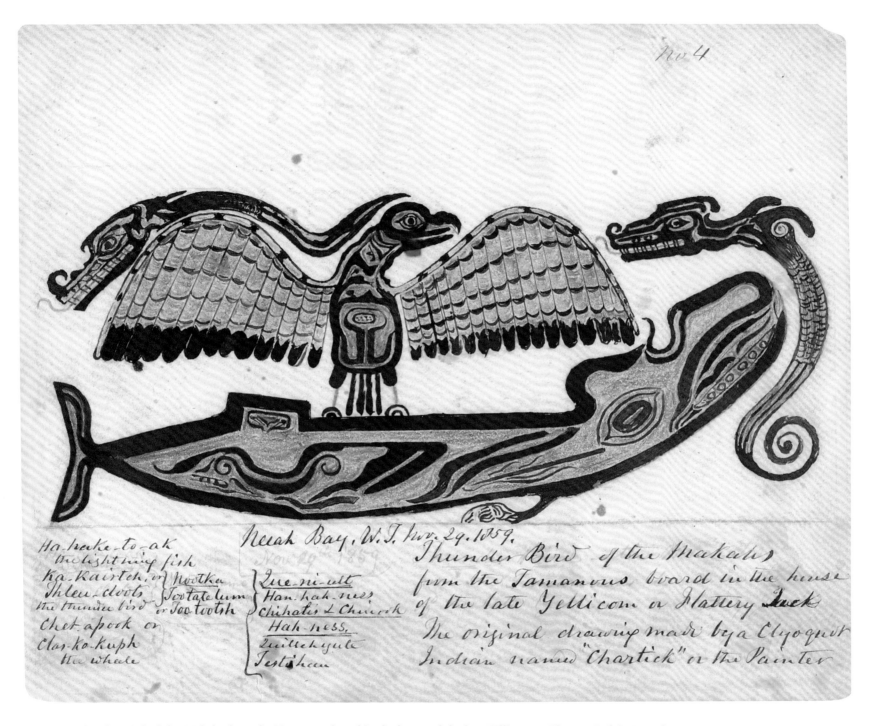

"Thunder Bird of the Makahs from the Tamanous board in the house of the late Yellicom or Flattery Jack." November 29, 1859. 18.1 x 23 cm.

No. 5

This drawing is the *tzum* or private mark of Kitchen-sum a Makah, and was drawn by him Nov. 10.59

This is the mark put on his hat — paddle canoe or any thing he wants to make his own.

The red paint is made of chewed salmon eggs, spit into vermillion the black is from ground bituminous coal.

Paint brush

Char-tioux, Painting
Char-tich — a Painter

"Kitchen-sum. Private mark."
November 10, 1859. 22.8 x 18.1 cm.

"Swells monument at Neeah Bay near Websters point
Swell killed march 1st 1861 monument built + completed Apr 1861"

"Tomahnawos board at the base of monument over 'Swell' a Makah chief buried at Baadah Pt. Neah Bay W.T." [April 1861 ?] 18 x 23.4 cm.

"Swells monument at Neeah Bay near Webster's Point. Swell killed March 1st 1861. Monument built and completed Apr. 1861." [April 1861 ?] 18.2 x 12.9 cm.

Timah natoos board at the base of monument ...
au Swell a makah chief — buried at Baadah Pt Neeah Bay W.S

"Grave of an Indian Woman at Baadah Neah Bay." November 1, 1859. 18.1 x 23 cm.

"Colchote's Lodge. Neeah Bay." March 20, 1861. 18.1 x 22.5 cm

"Baadah Point, Neah Bay" 18.5 x 22.6 cm.

"Tsiahk or Medicine Dance. Makah Indians, Neah Bay." 1861. 17.2 x 23.4 cm.

"Tsiark - or medicine dance of the Makahs.
Womans dress front view" February 5, 1863.
21.8 x 15.0 cm.

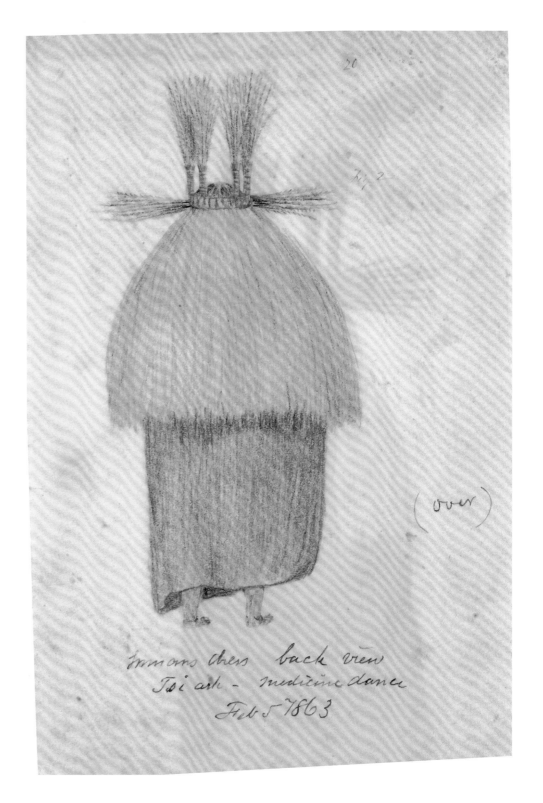

"Tsiark - or medicine dance of the Makahs.
Womans dress back view." February 5, 1863.
21.8 x 15.0 cm.

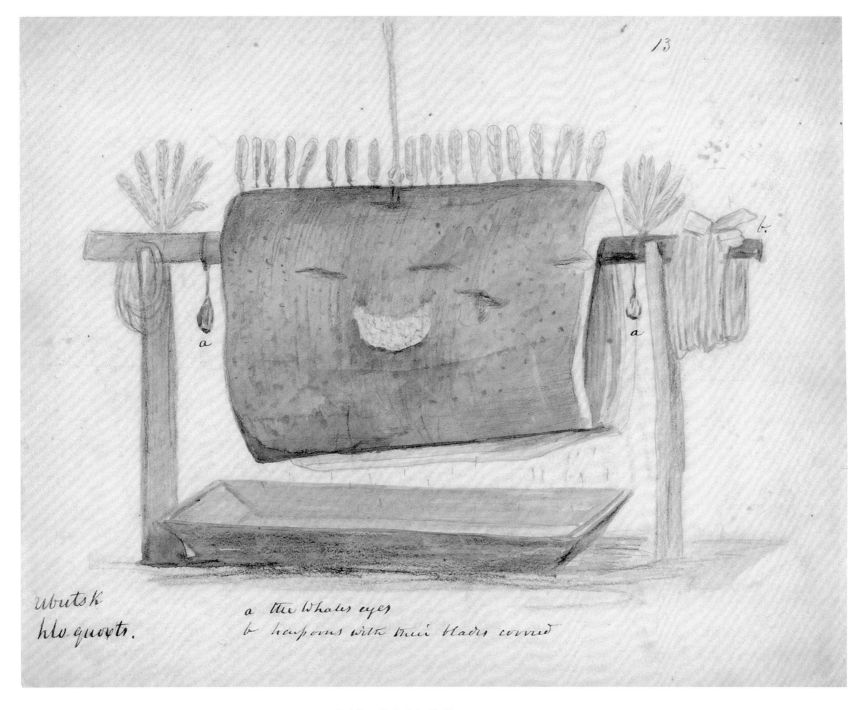

Saddle of whale's blubber. 18 x 23 cm.

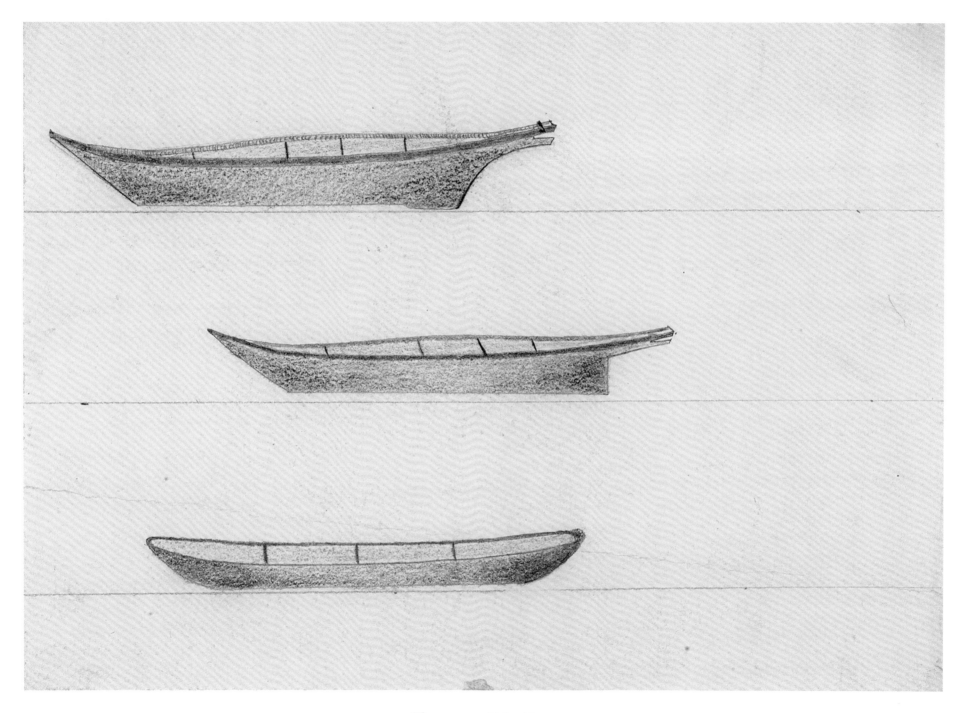

Three canoes. 26.5 x 19 cm.

"Baada Village. Baada Point, or Bahada Pt., Neah Bay." 1862. 17.8 x 25.1 cm.

Unidentified white house. 1865. 18.4 x 22.5 cm.

"View of Entrance to Quillehuyt Harbor." July 30, 1861. 18 x 23 cm.

No 1   Cape Flattery from Tatoosh Island no

"Cape Flattery from Tatoosh Island." [July 1861 ?] 17.7 x 25.2 cm.

Kiddle cubbut village
between Neah Bay and
Cape Flattery Wash.

Perilous position of HBM's Steamer Hecate
in the summer of 1861

"Perilous position of HBM's Steamer *Hecate* in the summer of 1861." 16.5 x 23.5 cm.

Fuca Pillar off Cape Flattery. 25 x 35 cm.

"Sugar loaf rock and arches under point of rocks on the beach between Tsooses and Hosett looking toward Flattery Rocks." October 1863. 16.5 x 19.3 cm.

Indian ceremonial dancer. [1863 ?] 19.3 x 16.5 cm.

"Hudson Bay Co. Post. Fort Simpson B.C." October 29, 1869. 17.6 x 25.4 cm.

"U S Military Post Tongass Alaska Ty." October 30, 1869. 17.5 x 25.5 cm.

Tattoos

Haida tattooing ceremony? 25.3 x 35 cm.

squid

thunderbird

sculpin

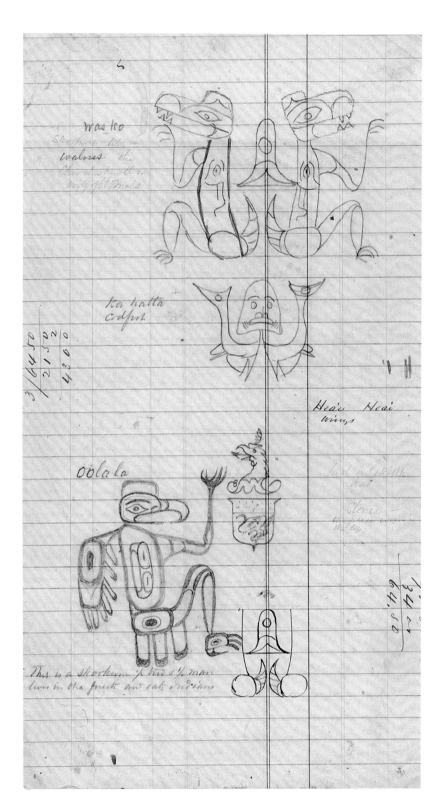

Sketches of Wasko, Kahalta, and Oolala (skookum) tattoos.
[May 1873 ?] 29.2 x 15.9 cm.

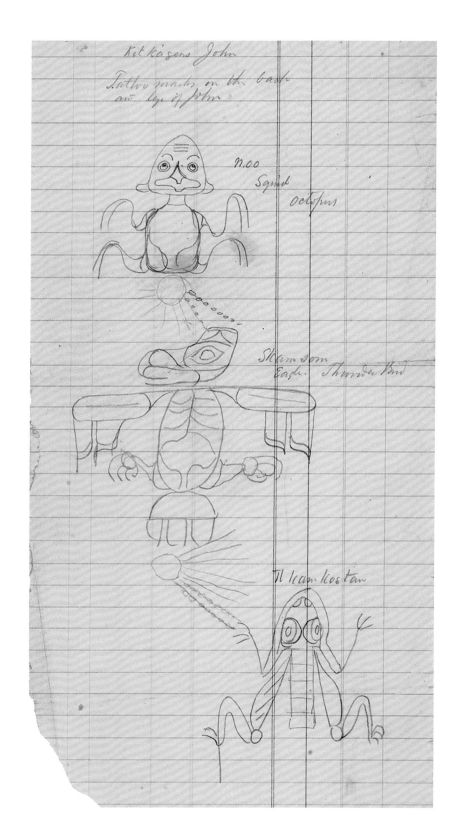

Tattoo marks on the back and legs of John Kitkagens.
[May 1873 ?] 40.6 x 15.8 cm.

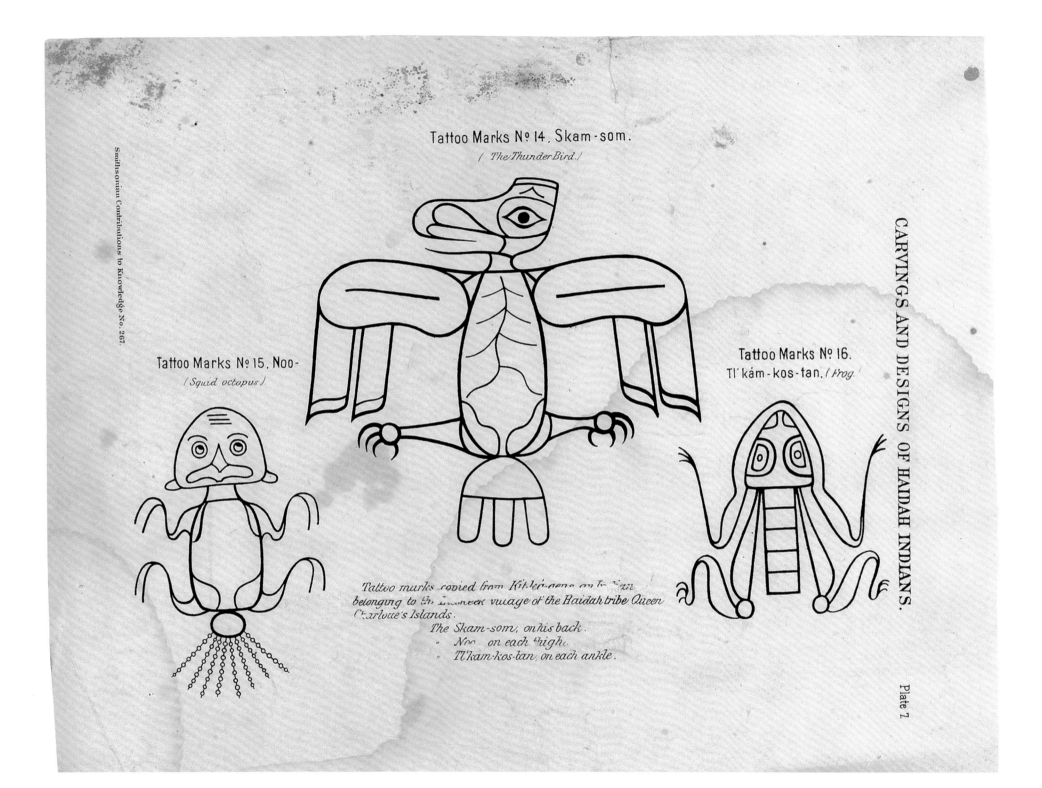

Tattoo Marks Nº 14. Skam-som.

(The Thunder Bird.)

Tattoo Marks Nº 15. Noo-

(Squid octopus.)

Tattoo Marks Nº 16.

Tl'kám-kos-tan. *(Frog.)*

Tattoo marks copied from Kit-ka-dens on Indian
belonging to the Skedeek village of the Haidah tribe Queen
Charlotte's Islands.
The Skam-som, on his back.
" Noo on each thigh.
" Tl'kam-kos-tan, on each ankle.

Plate 7

"Haida Indians of Queen Charlotte Island B.C."
February 9, 1879. 24.8 x 19.5 cm.

"Tattoo marks. No. 14 Skam-som
(The Thunderbird). Plate 7
from *The Haidah Indians
of Queen Charlotte's Islands,
British Columbia....* 1874.
23.6 x 29.8 cm.

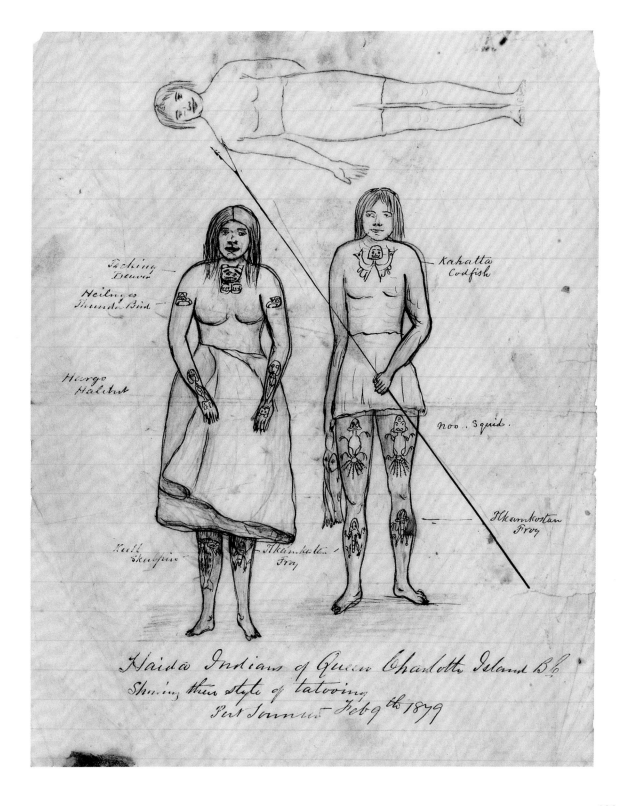

"Nittinat Indians tattoo marks." January 20, 1881 29.3 x 31.5 cm.

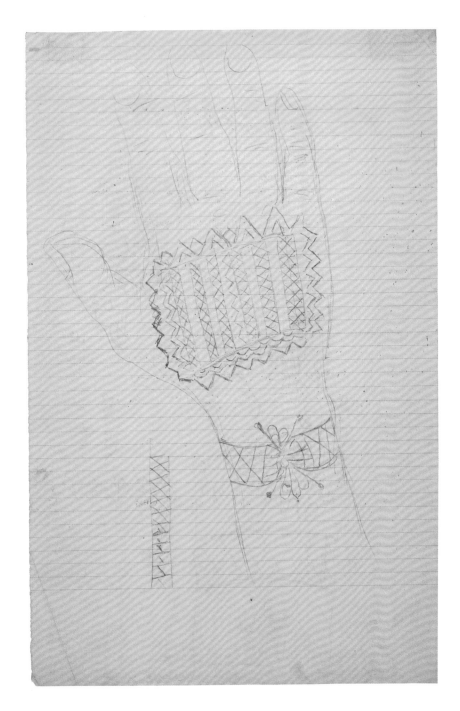

"Nittinat Indians tattoo marks." January 20, 1881. 29.3 x 31.5 cm.

Neah Bay Revisited

Seal club. August 25, 1879. 25.2 x 35.1 cm.

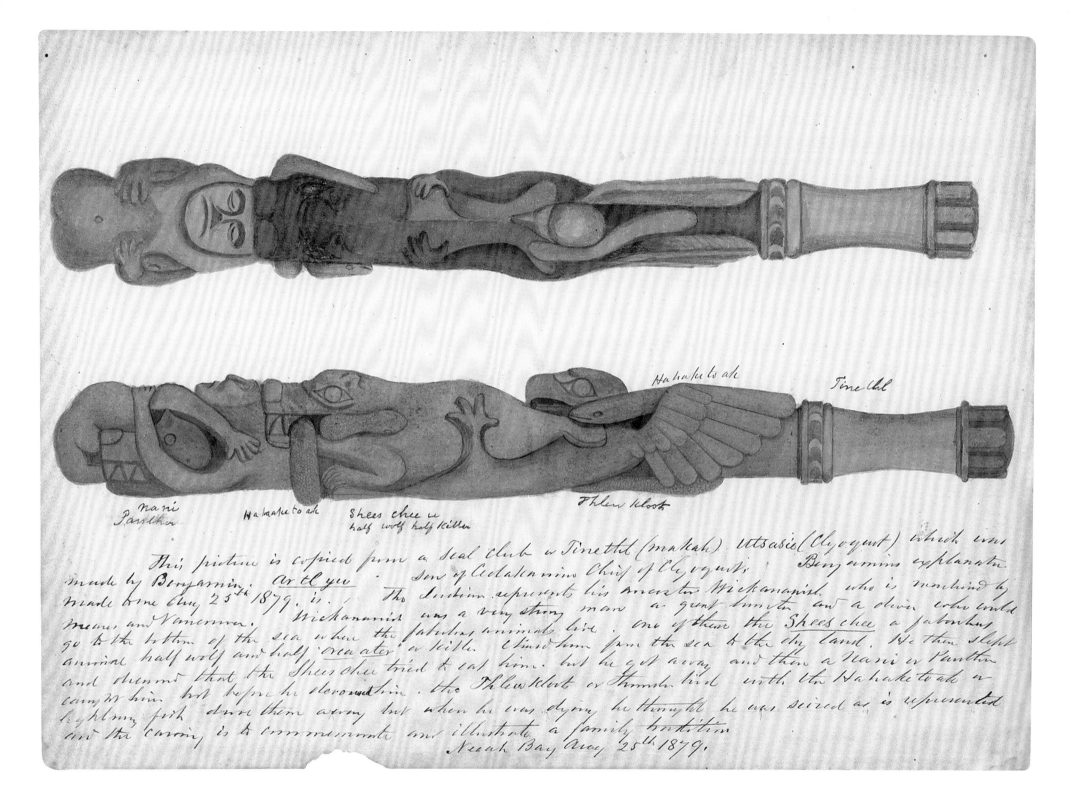

Nani
Panther

Hahaketoah

Shees chee u
half wolf half Killer

Fhlew Kloot

Hahaketoah

Tinethl

This picture is copied from a seal club a Tinethl (makah) Uttsasis (Clyoquit) which was made by Benjamin Artlyeu son of Cedakennino Chief of Clyoquits. Benjamins explanation made one aug. 25th 1879 is. The Indian represents his ancestor Wickananish who is mentioned by means and Vancouver. Wickananish was a very strong man a great hunter and a diver who could go to the bottom of the sea where the fabulous animals live. One of them the Shees chee a fabulous animal half wolf and half orca ater a Kittle. Chased him from the sea to the dry land. He then slept and observed that the Shees chee tried to eat him. but he got away and there a Nani or Panther carry in him but before he devoured him. the Thlew Kloot or thunder bird with the Hahaketoah a lightning fork drove them away but when he was dying he thought he was seized as is represented and the carving is to commemorate and illustrate a family tradition.
Neeah Bay aug. 25th 1879.

Spearhead. 20 x 31.6 cm.

Spearheads. [1881 ?] 20 x 26.2 cm.

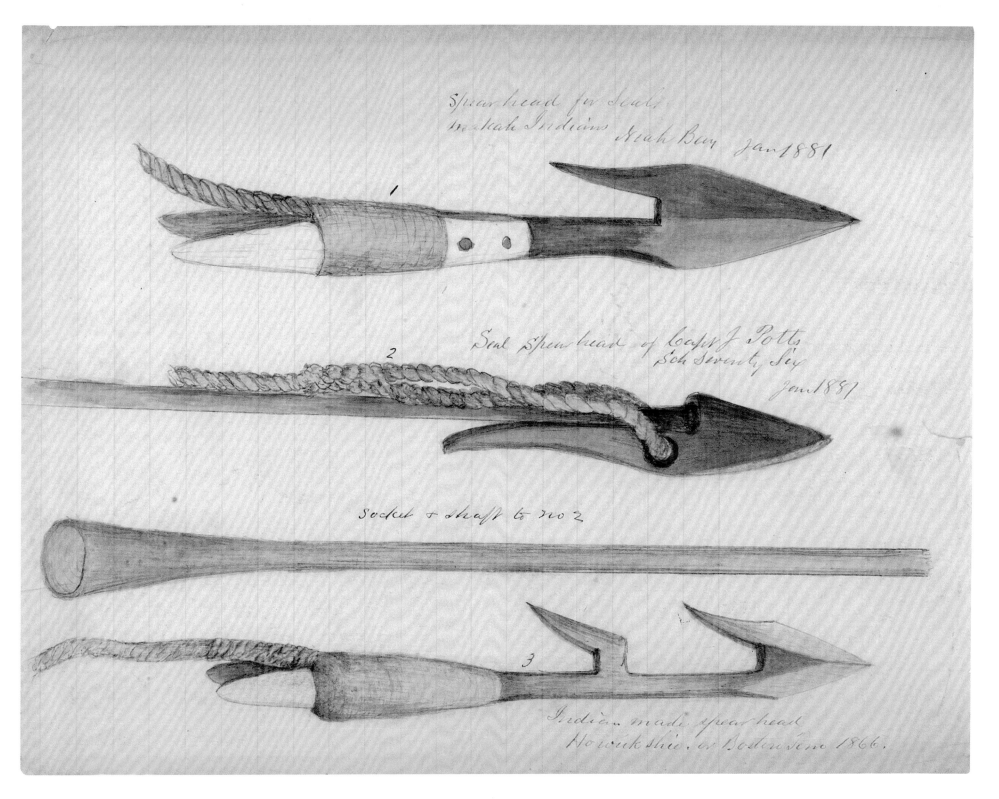

Spearhead for Seals
Meekah Indians Neah Bay Jan 1881

Seal Spear head of Capt J Potts
Sch Seventy Six
Jan 1881

Socket & Shaft to no 2

Indian made spear head
Howikshie or Boston Jem 1866.

Drawing of Cape Flattery and Fuca pillar. 20.5 x 27.4 cm.

"Cape Flattery W.T., Tsatsardadi rock or Fuca Pillar." May 18, 1881. 17.6 x 25.1 cm.

Half-stereo photograph of buildings
at Neah Bay. 8.8 x 7.8 cm.

"Home of J.G. Swan, Neah Bay Indian Reservation,
Wash. Terr." 20.3 x 28.6 cm.

House. 17.5 x 25.4 cm.

"Cape Flattery Light House & Fog Signal, Tatoosh Island W.T." May 1881. 17.8 x 25.1 cm.

The Queen Charlotte Islands

"House and carved column of Anneth las[?]
a chief at Massett Charlotte Islands B.C."
July 19, 1883. 35.1 x 25.3 cm.

Hooyeh the Raven at the bottom
The Raven as a man is holding the Magic Salmon
Tsia, which bites out the ravens heart and he
remains a Raven ever afterwards.
Above the Raven is the (Hoorts) Bear with the
Winter (Towats) in his mouth, and his
claws tearing upon the Winters breast.
The upper figure is a Bear of Hoorts, with two
frogs, one of which he is eating.
The three small figures surmounting all
are the chief, in centre, and two friends
with the Tadn skillih, a hat of
ermine on their heads.

House and carved columns amethlees a chief
at Massett, Queen Charlotte Islands B.C.
J.G. Swan   del July 14th 1883

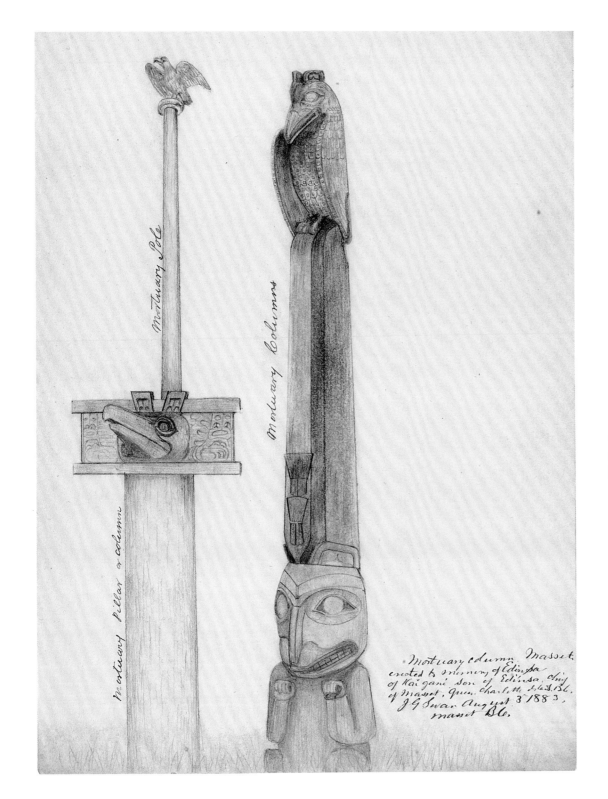

Mortuary Pole

Mortuary Columns

Mortuary Pillar or column

Mortuary column. Massett.
erected to memory of Edinsa
of Kaigani Son of Edinsa, chief
of Massett. Queen charlotte Islands. B.C.
J.G. Swan August 3 1883,
Massett B.C.

"Mortuary column, Masset. Erected to memory
of Edinso of Kaigani son of Edinso, Chief of Masset,
Queen Charlotte Island, B.C." August 3, 1883. 35.1 x 25.2 cm.

"Haida canoe as seen at
Massett Queen Charlotte Island."
July 1883. 18 x 24.5 cm.

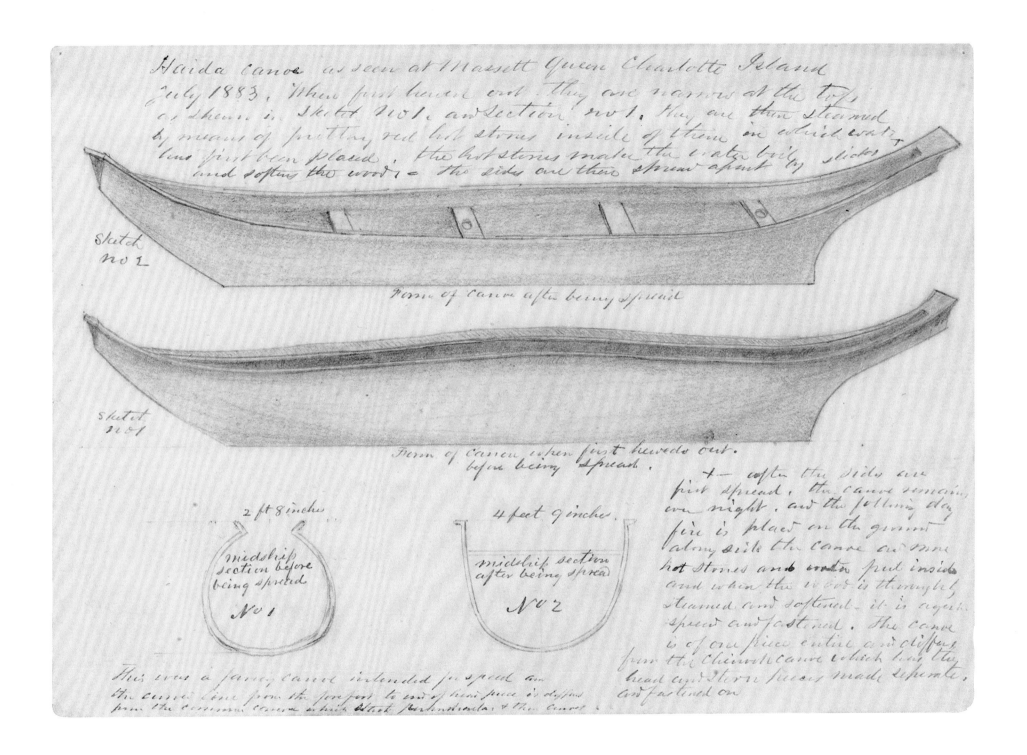

Haida canoe as seen at Massett Queen Charlotte Island
July 1883. When first hewed out they are narrow at the top,
as shewn in sketch No 1. and section No 1. they are then steamed
by means of putting red hot stones inside of them in which water
has first been placed. the hot stones make the water boil, slicker
and softens the wood — the sides are then shrew apart +

Sketch
No 2

Form of canoe after being spread

Sketch
No 1

Form of canoe when first hewed out.
before being spread.

2 ft 8 inches

midship
section before
being spread
No 1

4 feet 9 inches.

midship section
after being spread
No 2

+ after the sides are
first spread, the canoe remains
one night, and the following day
fire is placed on the ground
along side the canoe an more
hot stones and water put inside
and when the wood is thoroughly
steamed and softened it is again
spread and fastened. the canoe
is of one piece entire and differs
from the Chinook canoe which has the
head and stern pieces made separate
and fastened on

This was a fancy canoe intended for speed an
the curved line from the forefoot to end of head piece is different
from the common canoe which start perpendicular & then curves.

Klatagewos or Pillar Rock on north end
of Graham Island Queen Charlotte group
a columnar mass of sandstone & conglomerate
about twenty five feet in diameter and ninety five
feet high the summit is sloping and covered with small
bushes

"Klatagewos or Pillar Rock on north end
of Graham Island Queen Charlotte group."
[August 1883] 25.5 x 18 cm.

"Edinso's house at Kioosta,
North end Graham Island, B.C."
August 12, 1883. 25.5 x 17.9 cm.

"Heraldic column of Kioosta village,
Parry Passage, Queen Charlotte Islands."
[August 1883] 25.5 x 18 cm.

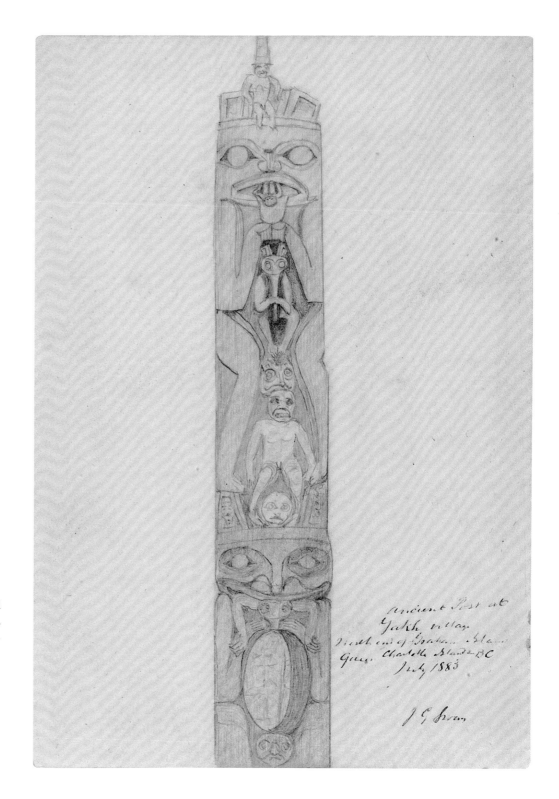

"Ancient Post at Yakh village, north end of Graham Island, Queen Charlotte Islands, B.C." [August 1883] 25.5 x 17.9 cm.

Tsetlat lints

Ancient Grave or burial house of a Skaga or doctor on a conglomerate boulder North Island B.C.

"Tsetlat Cints[?], ancient grave or burial house of a Skaga or doctor on conglomerate boulder, North Island, B.C." [August 1883] 25.6 x 18 cm.

"Ancient Totem column embedded in a spruce tree found at ancient village of Chathl in E. coast North Island." August 11, 1883. 25.5 x 18 cm.

Tchimose

dragon fly

Skatun Kelp   Thlkama kelp   kelp

koo kooltakook – Centipede   mouse
                              owl keotkoonali

Hoorts – Bear

Hunlo

Heraldic and totemic column
or Picturegraph in front of house at
Skidegate Q C Islands BC   J G Swan del.
                                aug 1883.

"Heraldic and totemic column or Picturograph
in front of house at Skidegate QC Island, BC."
August 1883. 25.4 x 18 cm.

"Chief Bear Skin's Indian House at Skidegate Queen Charlotte Islands, B.C. with carved images of Judge Pemberton of Victoria as objects of ridicule." [August 1883] 25.4 x 18.1 cm.

"Kitkuns house, Laskeek, Queen Charlotte Island, B.C."
September 7, 1883. 25.5 x 18 cm.

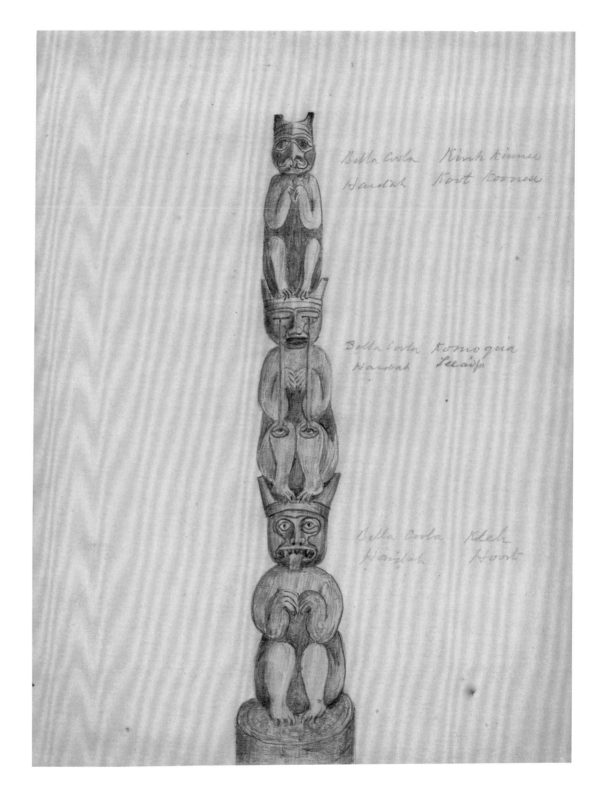

"Bella Coola, Haidah." 27.3 x 20.9 cm.

"Legend of the Three Hunters and the Bear." 20.9 x 27.1 cm.

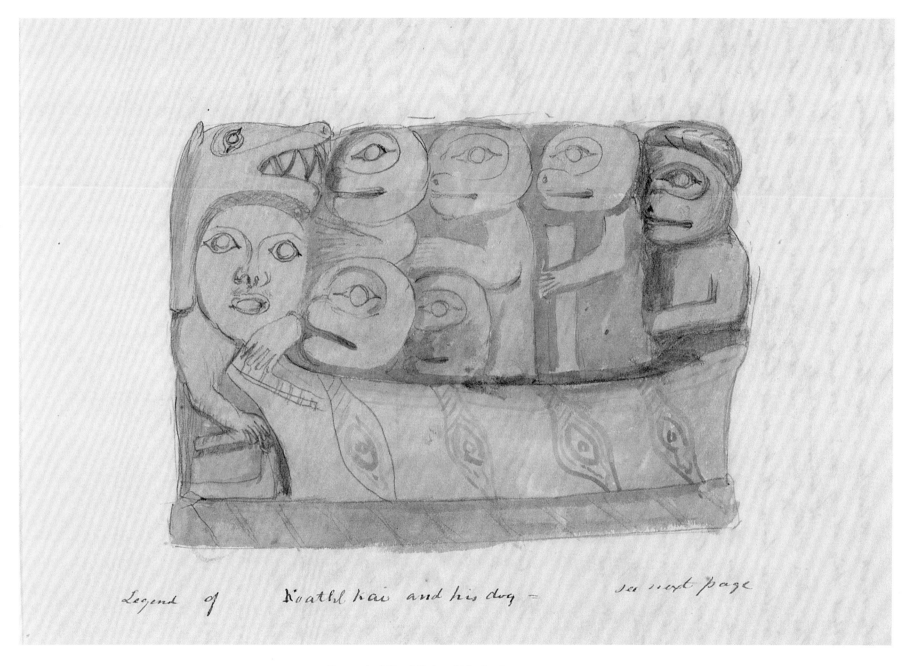

"Legend of Koathlkai and his dog." 20.8 x 26.8 cm.

Works by Johnny Kit Elswa

"Raven (Hooyeh) in Whale (Koone).
Haida mythology." 1883. 17.7 x 25.5 cm.

Raven, (Hooyeh) in whale, (Koone)
Haida mythology
drawn by Johnny Kit Elswa, Interpreter to
J G Swan 1883

Hooyeh the Raven

Haida Mythology.

Drawn by Johnny Kit Elswa Interpreter to J G Swan 1883

Hous kana the fisherman

"Hooyeh the Raven. Hous kana the fisherman. Haida mythology." 1883. 18 x 25.5 cm.

Skana. the killer (orca)   Haida mythology

Drawn by Johnny Kit Elswa Interpreter to J. G. Swan

Massett QCI 1883.

"Skana the killer (orca). Haida mythology." 1883. 17.9 x 25.5 cm.

Raven Hooyeh   Bella Coola
       Chimose   combination
Whale Skana
         Johnny Kit Elswa
         April 20 1887

"Raven" and "Whale," 1881. 24 x 29.1 cm.

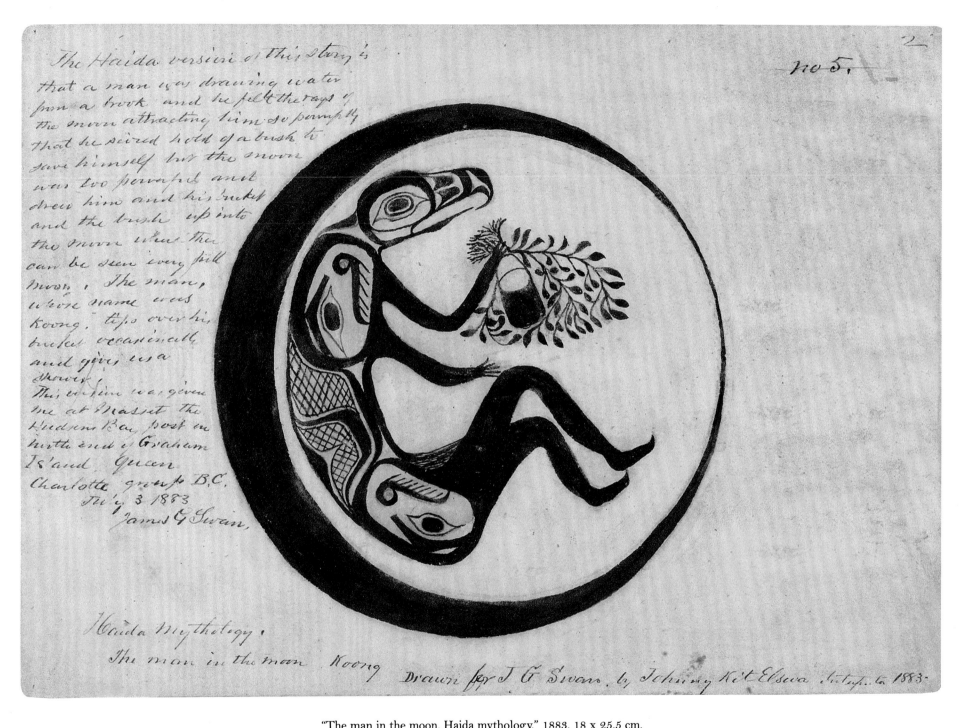

The Haida version of this story is that a man was drawing water from a brook and he felt the rays of the moon attracting him so powerfully that he seized hold of a bush to save himself but the moon was too powerful and drew him and his bucket and the bush up into the moon where they can be seen every full moon. The man, whose name was Koong, tips over his bucket occasionally and gives us a shower.

This volume was given me at Massit the Hudsons Bay post on north end of Graham Island, Queen Charlotte group B.C.
July 3 1883
James G Swan,

Haida Mythology.
The man in the moon Koong

Drawn for J G Swan, by Johnny Kit Elswa Antiquity to 1883

"The man in the moon. Haida mythology." 1883. 18 x 25.5 cm.

"Tekul or cirrus clouds" 1883. 17.9 x 25.5 cm.

"Hooyeh"

Heraldic Raven of the Haida Indians. Queen Charlotte Islands, B.C.

Drawn by Johnny Kit Elswa, Interpreter to J G Swan 1883

"Hooyeh: Heraldic Raven of the Haida Indians. Queen Charlotte Islands, B.C." 1883. 18 x 25.5 cm.

Wasko,

A mythological marine animal, part bear and part 'killer' (orca) Totem of Haida Indians Queen Charlotte Islands B.C.

Drawn by Johnny Kit Elswa Interpreter to J.G Swan 1883

"Wasko. A mythological marine animal part bear and part 'killer' (orca). Totem of Haida Indians, Queen Charlotte Islands, B.C." 1883. 18 x 25.5 cm.

"Skulpin Kul." 1883. 17.9 x 25.5 cm.

"Kahalta. Dog fish." 1883. 18 x 25.5 cm.

"Koot. Sparrow Hawk on its Nest." 1883. 18 x 20.5 cm.

Marine Life

"Black Cod." July 3, 1884. 18 x 25.5 cm.

Black Cod.

Pollachius Chalcogrammus Bean —   Coal fish,

Anoplopoma fimbria, Jordan,

Black Cod from Cape Flattery
                              Depth 8½ inches
        July 3ᵈ 1884 Length 43 inches
                       weight 21 pounds

K'thlumma Clallam —

"Beshow" Makah —

"Skil" Haida — "Kwakoolth" Bella Bella.

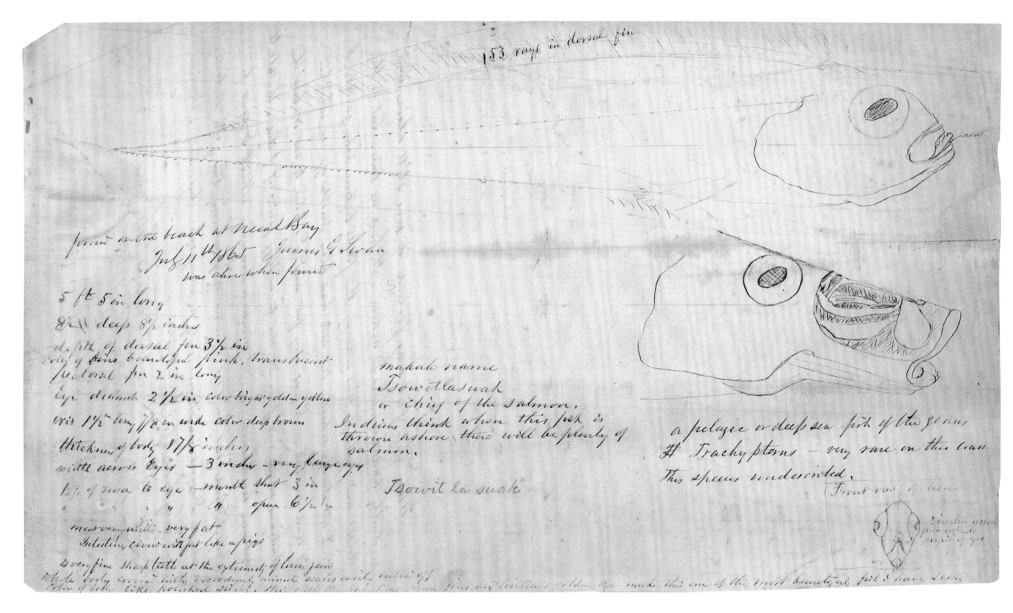

"A pelagic or deep sea fish of the genus Trachyptorus." July 11, 1865. 18 x 23 cm.

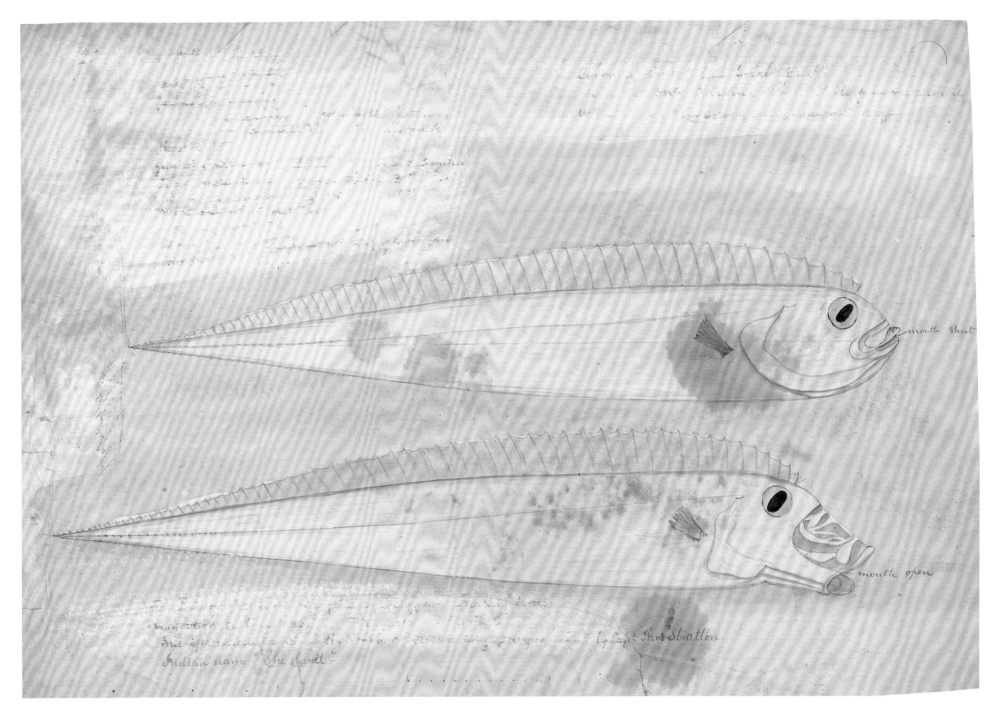

"Indian name She shoutl(?)" 23.8 x 34.5 cm.

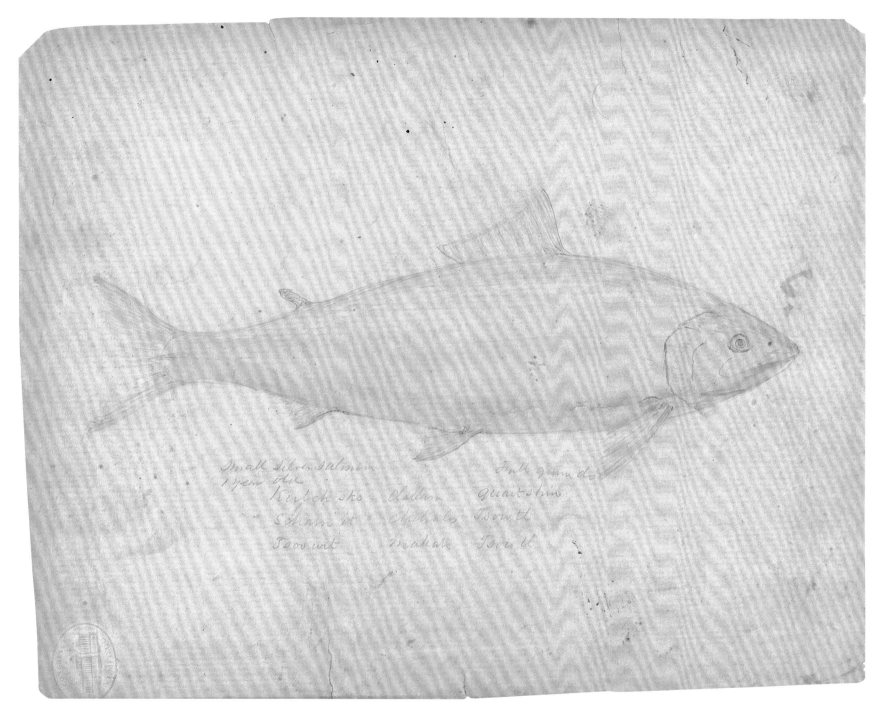

"Small silver salmon, one year old." 18.5 x 32.4 cm.

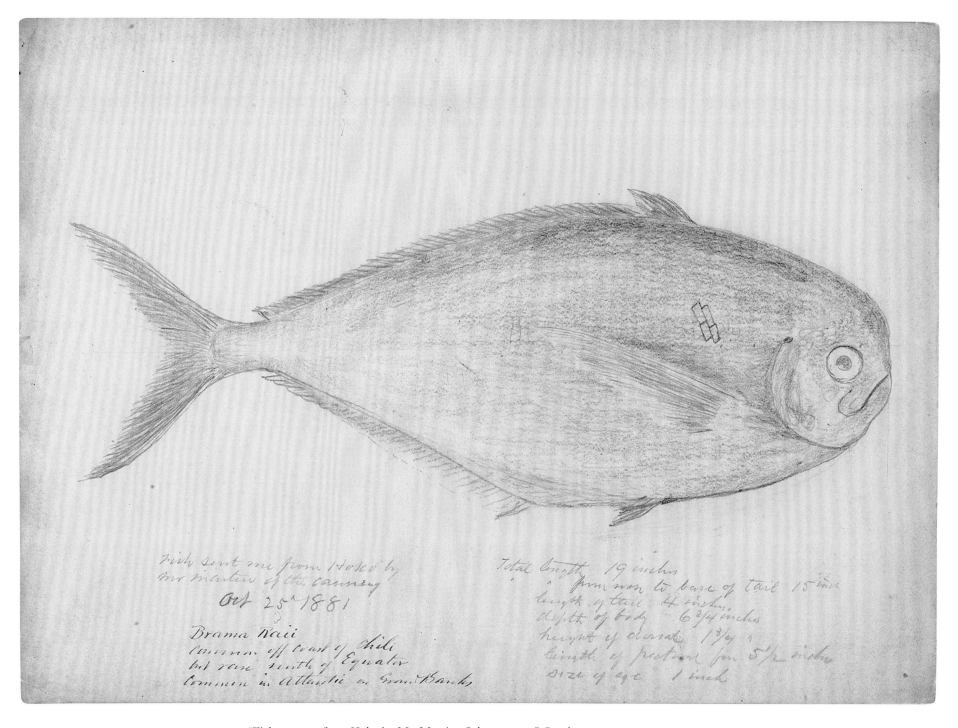

"Fish sent me from Hoko by Mr. Martin of the cannery." October 25, 1881. 25.2 x 35.1 cm.

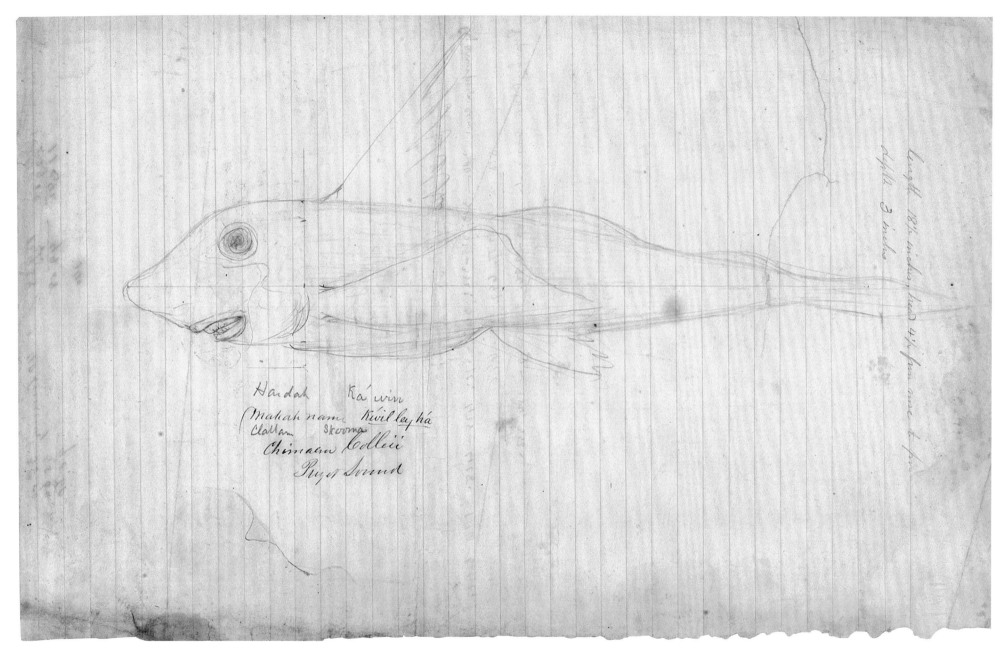

Hardah   Ká'win
(Makah name Kúvil leyhá
Clallam   Skoomg
Chimaera Colleii
Puget Sound

length 18½ inches head 4½ from mouth to fin
till to 3 inches

"Chimaera Colleii, Puget Sound." 19.5 x 31.8 cm.

"Sta hum[?] – Haida." 25.2 x 35 cm.

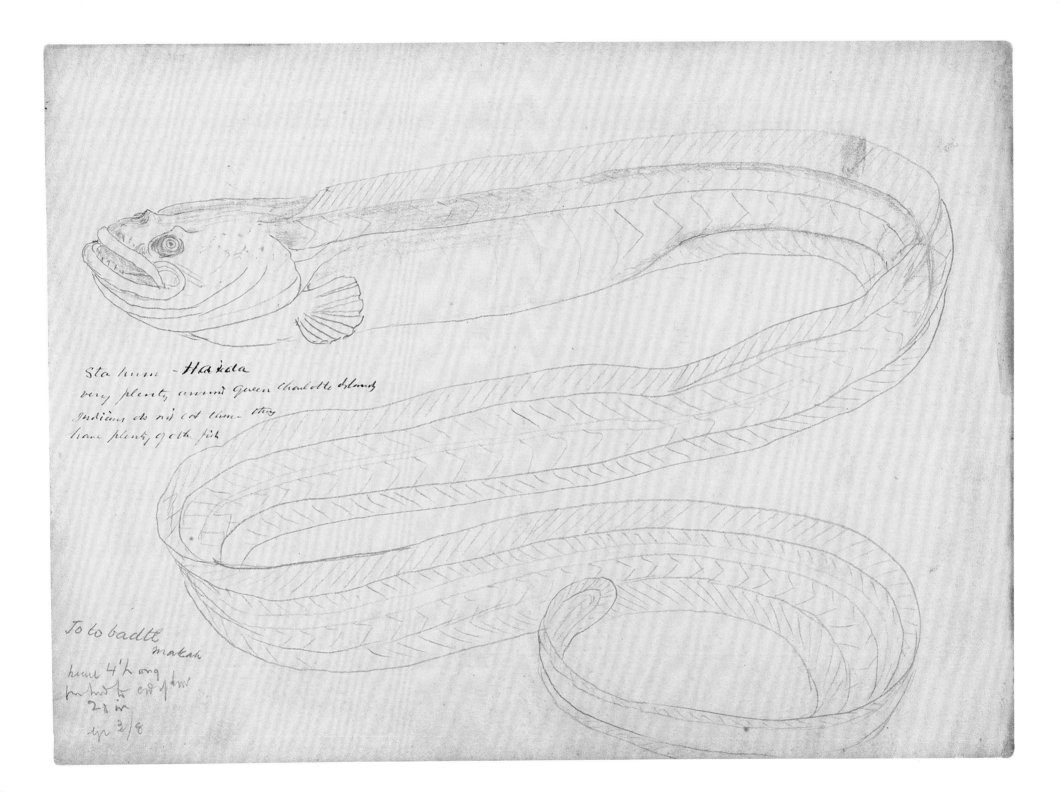

Sta hum - Haida
very plenty, around Queen Charlotte Islands
Indians do not eat them they
have plenty of oth fish

To to badtt
        makah
hunl 4' h ong
finheod fo end of tenr
    21 in
    eye 3/8

Rough Sketches

"Salmon fishing on Chinook Beach." 13.1 x 20.6 cm.

"Quilleyute, Wash." 17.7 x 25.2 cm.

Unidentified coastal village. 14.2 x 22.8 cm.

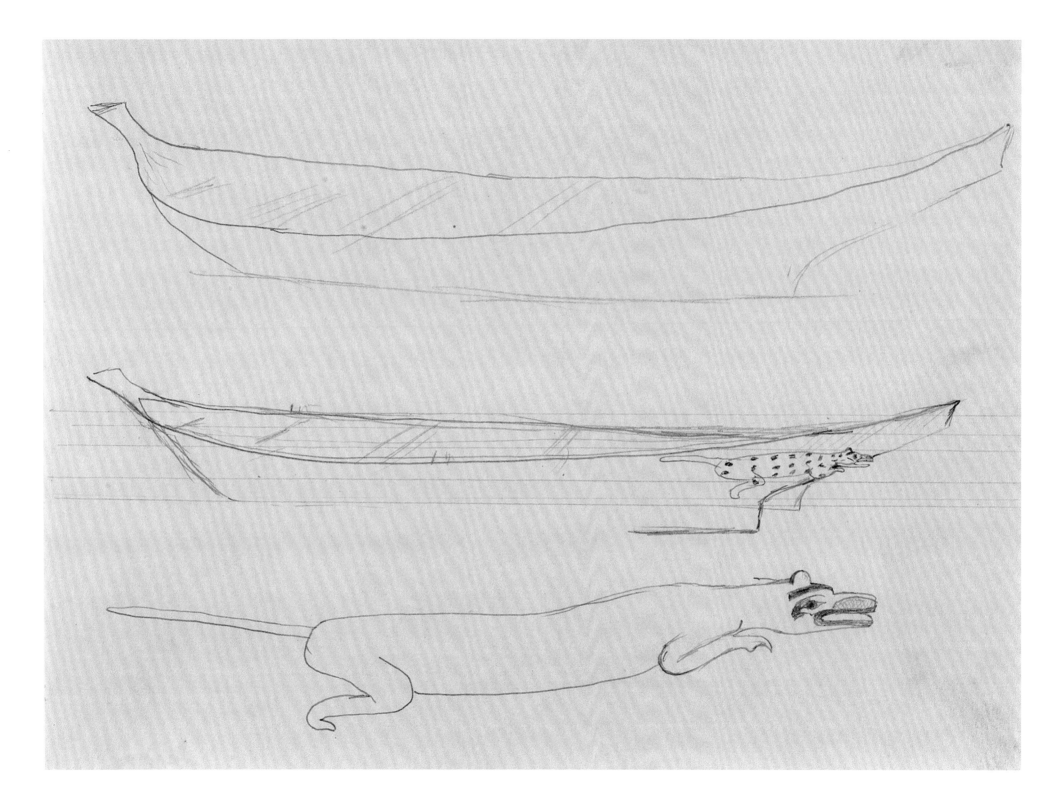

Totem pole. 25.5 x 17.9 cm.

Canoes and ornaments. 20.5 x 27.4 cm.

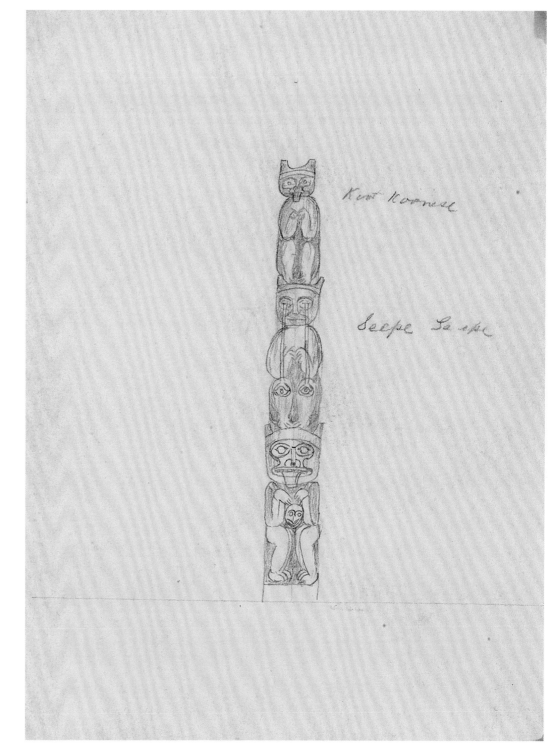

Rough sketches of Indian ceremonial dancers. [1863 ?] 19.3 x 33 cm.

"Indian Boy - seen on Barclay Sound in a little schooner rigged boat dug out of a log - about
3 feet long by 18 inches wide - Boy about 6 years old." 14.1 x 17.4 cm.

Design GREER ALLEN · *Color separations* PROFESSIONAL GRAPHICS, INC.

Printing THAMES PRINTING COMPANY · *Binding* ACME BOOKBINDING COMPANY